I0409509

SIC FIGS INVESTMENT STRATEGIES FOR BEGINNERS

Third edition

Donald Smyth

Copyright © 2024 Donald Smyth

All rights reserved

No part of this book may be reproduced, or stored in a retrieval system,
or transmitted in any form or by any means, electronic, mechanical,
photocopying, recording, or otherwise, without express written permission
of the publisher.

ISBN-13: 9798862233315
ISBN-10: 1477123456

Cover design by: Sic Figs (Logo by Studio Foranda)
Library of Congress Control Number: 2018675309
Printed in the United States of America

*To all of the working class dogs out there who
would rather be a capitalist pig instead*

CHAPTER 1: DOLLARS TO DOUGH NOTS

It was all the way back in the spring of 2006 when the idea for trading individual stocks began to creep around inside of my head for the first time. Although, the thought of bettering my financial position had definitely begun to germinate even before that. Back in the summer of 2003, I traveled from Boston to Key West with my fiancé to visit with family. It was during that trip that I first began to seriously start thinking about the finer things in life, and how I wanted to start getting in on a piece of that action for myself. Courtesy of an intervention of fate, the culprit for this eureka moment was an advertisement, of all things. Believe it or not, this new way of thinking all began with the perusal of a magazine that I had picked up in an airport newsstand to pass the time spent between flying and waiting and waiting and flying, a periodical dedicated to a preview of the upcoming football season, to be exact. Surreptitiously adorning the back cover of that particular magazine was a full-page ad for the Rolex Submariner diving watch, a status symbol of wealth and privilege that I had not had the privilege to become intimately familiar with at the time. And for good reason.

I had grown up as the middle child in a middle class family that seemed entirely too comfortable and disturbingly numb about the prospects of going about their business as working class slaves to the grind. One of my ancestors had been President of the United States of America (it was James Garfield) and my own grandfather had been the wealthy president of Stanley Woolen

Mills. My father was raised on a nine acre estate containing a fifteen-room main house, a guest house, a carriage house, three car garage, horse stables, a pool and pool house sitting on top of a hill from which the children would ski down in the winter. The property also had its own pond, and was surrounded by the standard of mid-century American idealism: The white picket fence. For depression-era America, it reeked of money and privilege, but that wealth was not generational in that it did not work its way down to me, or even my father for that matter. The fortune was ultimately too small to be any kind of legacy advantage to the generations that came after, due in large part to the fact that my grandfather had nine children, at least one mistress, a sailboat and a penchant for otherwise having a good time with his fortune. I did get to spend some time in the house though, so you would think that I should have been impressed upon at an early age about the perks and benefits of having versus having not. It is certainly true that I got the opportunity to see life from both sides, his and mine. For whatever the reason, it didn't register in my thinking at the time. As such, I spent my early adult years toiling as a grocery clerk in a neighborhood supermarket, courtesy of the fact that my parents had not prepared me to be a success. Indeed, they seemed oblivious to the possibility that anyone could be something more than a working class dog, punching a time clock and working for "The Man," satisfying their wants and needs with a few crumbs from the table of life. It didn't help matters that my father was a mentally unstable drunk and that my mother had a sixth grade education. Real success was not in their wheelhouse. They didn't know it personally, they didn't understand it intuitively and they didn't know how to foster it or make it their reality. As a result, my younger self was screwed! At least initially that is, as evidenced by the fact that I never made more than $18,500 per year when I was trying to make a living as an unskilled laborer. Because of this, I largely lacked the life experience that might have put me in the know regarding Rolex and their fine line of luxury watches. This is especially true when you consider that the only rich person that I had a tie to (my grandfather) died when I was only four years old. The name Rolex doesn't go hand-in-hand with the occupation of grocery clerk, and they especially do not pair well on that kind of a salary. Accordingly, I had never previously given a cursory nod or even a second thought to owning one someday. It simply wasn't the world that I was accustomed to traveling in. But that didn't stop me from wanting one when I saw it adorning the back page of that magazine for the very first time.

Oh man, it was beautiful! I remember being instantly captivated by the aesthetic of its design, with its striking blue face and bezel, trimmed out with 18 karat gold, its two-toned gold and stainless steel wristband. Stunning!

The Rolex Submariner diving watch. Wanting to buy this watch and not having the discretionary funds to do so is what got me thinking about ways to do better financially.

I became obsessed with the idea of getting one, and I thought about it constantly. I even found myself fixating on the image conveyed in that advertisement on more than a few occasions as the week progressed. I was totally enraptured by it, and I wanted one *so, so* badly. The only problem was that I wasn't rich at the time by any standard of measure, and Rolex is more or less a status symbol of wealth and success. They were something that rich people wore. Not Average Joe people with Average Joe salaries.

By this time, I was a college educated medical professional who was doing alright, but not THAT alright. Buying a luxury watch like the Rolex Submariner seemed like a bridge too far to me at that moment in time, an idea better relegated to the realm of fantasy and maybe someday. Then, on our last night in Key West, as we strolled down the local tourist trap, I saw that very same watch in person, in the window of a local jeweler, and it stopped me dead in my tracks. I immediately went inside to take a closer look.

"I'm just here to look at it," I assured the sales associate.

I didn't want to give the wrong impression or suggest any false hopes regarding my intention to buy one, even as he was super nice and accommodating all the same, taking the watch out from under the glass counter so that I could see it better, suggesting that I try it on.

"Take all the time that you need," he said to me, as my girlfriend and I sat on the other side of the display case.

It was beautiful, even more so than it was in print. My heart raced as I tried it on and admired how it looked on my wrist. It was $6,200, and for a half hour I sat there and thought about it. I could have purchased it without too much difficulty. All that I had to do was to put it on a credit card and pay it off in installments stretching over a year or so, but I was set to marry my fiancé in less time than that and it seemed like an irresponsible expenditure of money considering our pending nuptials, which was set to include a two week stay in Hawaii.

"Do whatever you want," said my girlfriend, encouragingly.

It was nice of her to be supportive of the idea, knowing how much that I wanted that watch, she undoubtedly had seen me staring at the ad during the week at times. I had certainly made it obvious, intentionally or not. But ultimately, I came to the conclusion that it would be too greedy of me to consider buying it at that particular time and spending that much money on myself when I knew that we had all these other expenses coming down the pike. Getting married isn't cheap! But today that same watch sells for $20,500 brand new. And there isn't a day that goes by that I don't have regret about not buying it for $6,200 when I had the chance. Other than selling my copy of The Amazing Spider-Man no. 1 in 1998 for $625, that may be the second biggest financial error in judgment that I ever made. As of this writing, my copy would have sold on the open market for about $8,000 if I still owned it. I had originally purchased it in 1988 for $200.

Collectibles such as comics, stamps, coins, old toys, antiques, pottery and fine works of art can all be an under-the-radar and fun way to invest discretionary capital. Just like stocks, each collectible has a market that determines the value of a given item based on demand. Collectibles can easily be bought and sold (just like stocks) through brick and mortar stores or on-line vendors and auctions .

Skip ahead to 2005. By this time, I had been in my new job for four years but had not signed up for my company sponsored 401K retirement benefit, because I foolishly didn't want to shrink my paycheck by having deductions taken out. When I finally got around to doing so, it became my first exposure to owning stocks in any capacity, as well as having exposure to the stock market in general. Once again, I fell in love and found myself checking the balance on my account every afternoon when the market closed, which really made no sense in the context of this kind of stock ownership, since the goal is to make money spread out over years of returns, if not decades. But it still had not occurred to me to invest in and own individual stocks. Owning mutual funds under the umbrella of a retirement vehicle that is pretty much managed for you is one thing, buying and selling the stocks of individual companies is another. The stock market seemed foreign, intimidating and confusing to me. Business was boring as far as I was concerned and listening to any discussion of it was as titillating as watching paint dry. Then I happened to see another ad, and all that changed. I was about to stumble upon a new obsession.

It all started one autumn morning back in 2006 when I went to get my oil changed. Sitting in the waiting area, I picked up a copy of Smart Money and began to flip through the pages. There, I scrolled past an ad for gold buffalo nickels. Once again, just like I had a few years earlier with the Rolex Submariner, I became enraptured by them. At $600 each, it didn't seem to be good value to me.

Every portfolio should hold at least 10% of its total assets in gold as a hedge against inflation and volatility in the market. Gold also has a long, reliable and established history as a store of wealth.

At the time, gold and silver were on their way to climbing to generational highs, but gold had been about $300/ounce only a few years earlier, so I thought it prudent to wait for the price to come down a little before I made my move. Of course, it didn't. It more than tripled from there, and so did the price of the nickles. While I waited for an opportunity that never came, I stumbled across an article on Yahoo Finance that argued that if you wanted to be in the gold space, then you should consider owning gold stocks, in place of owning the physical metal. It listed about five or so of the best gold miners for consideration, so I set about doing a little research into each company. Barrick Gold piqued my interest, so with some money that I cashed out of my vacation bank, I bought twenty-eight shares of ABX. In short order, my investment returned double digits.

'Wow, that was easy,' I thought, somewhat naively. Nonetheless, I was hooked.

After that, buying stocks and building wealth became the main focus of my aspirations. It dominated my thinking. I was convinced that this was my ticket, my way out of wishing and hoping. I began to consume large volumes of media dedicated to the subject in the form of tv programs, books, periodicals and internet media. It was my all consuming passion, my "golf" so to speak. Only instead of hitting a ball around the fairway, I hit the charts, searching for opportunities. Stock charts, that is. I set about trying to learn as much as I could about the subject of investing, pouring over anything that I thought might be able to give me a leg up in the performance department. I was determined from that moment on that I was going to become a millionaire, and I absolutely would not accept any other outcome. I was not going to get left behind again. Like the day when I walked out on buying that Rolex, because I wasn't "rich" enough to take it home with me.

CHAPTER 2: IF IT AIN'T SIC, THEN IT'S JUST SICK

There are a lot of ill conceived notions populating the thoughts and sentiments of a generation who have come to view money and the accumulation of wealth as the source of all of society's problems and shortcomings. Wage inequality, corporate greed, wealth taxes and a growing call for socialism are the distraction for a thinly veiled and misplaced jealousy that would have you believe that "money doesn't buy you happiness." But let's cut out the bull-crap and stick to the facts. There are invariably and without question many factors that go into determining one's level of happiness and satisfaction, but this is not a book on the philosophy of life in general, this is a book about making money by investing in the stock market, so we are going to focus our attention on the financial side of this argument. It is an inarguable fact of life in my opinion, and this is the ground upon which I'm planting my flag, that it is always better to be on the richer side of things than it is to be poor, and anyone who tells you differently is either lying to themselves or lying to you in order to disingenuously make you feel better about your own unenviable situation. Let's start with the obvious, and that is that having money allows you to be miserable on your own terms, without adding to the mix the worry of where you're going to get your next meal from or lay your head at night. Every living creature needs two things in order to survive. Food and shelter. And unless you want to live in a wigwam and catch and butcher your own food, then that means money. That's probably a big reason why the notion that "money doesn't buy you happiness" has never prompted a single rich person from ever giving their wealth away in its entirety and while they were still alive and in need of the protection that it inherently provides (No fictional references needed, thank you!). Sure, some will make provisions to give it away after they are gone sometimes, but never while they are alive and still in need of it.

You know why?

Because money is a direct measure of the security and comfort that you enjoy in life. It is POWER, CHOICE and FREEDOM quantified. It is the ability to live life on your own terms with the least amount of compromise necessary, and the more money that you have, the more likely that mantra is to be the truth that you live by. Having financial stability puts you in a position to feel better about yourself and your surroundings. There is real value attached to knowing that you have a greater level of autonomy and control over the things that affect your quality of life. Wealth is the ultimate security blanket, but it is more than just security, comfort and being able to afford to buy whatever you want, whenever you want. It is the key to opening doors of opportunity that otherwise would not be available to you. Money gets you preferential treatment, and don't pretend that it doesn't or that there is something wrong with that. Human beings are only equal to a degree in terms of work ethic, determination, perseverance, grit and intelligence. Maybe you're not satisfied with being equal. You shouldn't be. Maybe you want a beach house or a cabin in the mountains where you can go to relax and unwind. Maybe you want to actually drive that exotic sports car that you've always dreamed about owning. Maybe you want to travel unencumbered by financial limitations. Maybe you don't want to work a 9 to 5 every day until the day that you die. Or maybe you just don't want to worry about how you're going to pay the rent or fix that old car of yours when it breaks down. Maybe you're someone who's willing to do something about it. The point is this: Money talks, and bullshit is working for a "living wage." That ain't living, and that's what Sic Figs and this book is all about. The power to live life on one's own terms, the multitude of choices that come with having money and the freedom to live life the way you see fit, that's what we're talking about here.

So what exactly is Sic Figs? Sic Figs is a social media investment ideas platform dedicated to celebrating the pursuit of wealth and the ancillary benefits of the better, safer and more secure tomorrow that having money can deliver. Sic Figs was launched in 2018 as a platform to illuminate investment strategies, identify opportunities brewing in the market, share those trade ideas with and inspire other like minded investors. Sic Figs highlights important financial news that may impact the market in general or specific stocks in particular, all while shamelessly espousing our unabashed support and enthusiasm for the pursuit of the six and seven lifestyle. Six figure incomes and seven figure portfolios. Because life was meant to be lived with the least amount of compromise possible. And let's face it, being poor just plain sucks! And so does worrying about not being able to afford what you want and need.

CHAPTER 3:
GRABBING THE BULL
BY THE HORNS

So, now we've covered Sic Figs philosophy on life and wealth and how they work together to allow you to live your best life, and that's what this book is all about, but what experiences rest behind the bull with the 6 strapped to its neck? Why should you pay heed to anything that this investment guide has to offer? The answer is simple. Been there, done that, and know better for having been down that road already. Sic Figs has been in your shoes if you've ever had to wait for a tax refund in order to afford to pay for something, and Sic Figs knows what it's like to not have those problems. Let's get a little personal and dig down into the specifics so you can better understand where I'm coming from. I started out my adult journey as a working class slave to the grind, working for a peasant wage that never amounted to more than $360 for a 56 hour work week. That was more than 30 years ago, but even when accounting for inflation, those numbers sucked even back then. That was no way to make a living and actually enjoy life. So, I went to college and got a bachelor's degree in science. That was step one in moving up in the world, but my finances got even worse after I graduated, at least initially, as I waited to get into a post-grad program, biding my time by working as a vet tech and a substitute teacher for a paltry and pathetic $17,000 per year.

That got your attention yet? The point that I'm trying to make is that when I speak about how having money can change your life for the better, I'm not just blowing smoke up your backside, I'm speaking from a position of experience. I know intimately well what it's like to not have money. Your opportunities are limited. The choices you have available to you are restricted by your lack of funds. The freedom that you have is curtailed and defined by what you can afford to do. Your desires are relegated to the unsatisfying status of hopes, dreams and maybe someday. And it's also true that you sometimes get treated with a higher degree of disregard and disrespect when you lack financial clout, because the lack of options that go hand-in-hand with a lack of money can put you in a position of weakness and leave you at the mercy of bosses, landlords and other people that you may not have otherwise needed to deal with. I've experienced it firsthand, so let's not pretend that those kinds of jerks aren't out there. I've worked enough crap jobs to know what I'm talking about. Unfortunately.

After working like a beast of burden through life for a decade, I got smart. I ditched the idea of becoming a veterinarian and switched to "human medicine" as a professional interest, where I started making a real salary for the first time in my life, one that wasn't embarrassing, anyways. As for my first foray into owning individual stocks, that began back in 2008. That first year, during the financial banking crisis and in the midst of the worst market sell off since the Great Depression, I dipped my toe into the market for the first time and scored a 42% return on my investment by timing my moves to perfection (admittedly, it was primarily just dumb luck, but it was enough to get my attention). The following year I returned 36%, followed by another 37% in 2010. Over the course of sixteen years of trading experience, I have returned 35% or more four times, had 10 double digit years of positive returns, 2 years of single digit positive returns and have lost money on 4 different occasions. My lifetime average yearly return stands at 13%, which is slightly higher than the S&P's historical average yearly return of 8-10%.

Take note that there were two years where my returns came

in particularly bad, at negative twenty-two and negative twenty-six percent. In both cases, I was caught being in the wrong place at the wrong time. One was my fault, and the other was the result of a broad market sell-off where I was heavy in the "out of favor" sector. The point is this, I've been right and I've been wrong. Every trade and every experience has been an opportunity to learn something about the market and how it works. I've soaked it all in over the course of sixteen years, the wins and especially the losses, because that's where you really take the best lessons from, all in the pursuit of becoming a better investor. For nearly two decades now, I have dedicated myself to the idea that power, choice and freedom are derived from opportunity that only wealth can provide. Because I know what it's like to not have money, and it's not how I want to live my life. If you disagree, then there's no problem with that either. There's no specific right or wrong to the question. Just be clear that there is probably no need for you to be reading this book if you feel differently. No judgment otherwise.

So, now that we've established beyond any reasonable doubt that I know at least a little something about being poor, how do you know that I've got experience on the other side of the equation? Here's where it gets a bit trickier. Never talk about or tell anyone how much money you have. That's Sic Fig's first rule in building a fat portfolio. I'll cover the particulars of that suggestion later in this book. But for now, let's just say that just like I know what it's like to be lower middle class, I know what it's like to not have those same worries. I know that doing better comes with its own set of advantages. It frees you up to experience more of the finer things in life. There is an inherent comfort that comes with not having to worry about every little thing that might go wrong or wonder how the hell you're going to pay for something if it does. There is security in the buffer that money places between you and the unexpected. It also gives you more control over the company that you keep, because when you're self-sufficient you can cut the toxic people out of your life, that maybe you once had to rely upon because you didn't have the financial option to stand alone. Just ask anyone who's ever been stuck in an abusive relationship because they didn't have the financial autonomy to do something about it. Can people still treat you poorly when you're rich? Sure they can. They can also kiss your seven figure portfolio on the way out the door as you're telling them good luck, goodbye and good riddance!

CHAPTER 4: WHO SHOULD USE THIS INVESTMENT GUIDE

In full disclosure, I am not a formally trained financial expert by any stretch of the imagination. I am a health professional with a baccalaureate degree in science by trade, harboring an abiding love for the stock market and making money on the side. I have been trading and investing successfully in the market for nearly twenty years. Sic Figs Investment Guide for Beginners is intended as an introduction to market basics for the novice investor just looking to get some exposure to buying and selling individual stocks for the first time. It is best suited to those individuals who have little or no knowledge of the stock market, by focusing on just those things that you need to know to get you started. Investing in stocks can be a confusing, convoluted and highly complex exercise. In this guide, we strive to keep things simple by focusing our effort on defining some basic market terminology, identifying what the stock market is all about, and going over some of the key strategies and philosophies that Sic Figs uses every day to successfully make money in the stock market. For starters, you should not be investing any money in the stock market that you can't afford to lose. That's akin to gambling and it's irresponsible. Picking stocks should never be a roll of the dice. Sic Figs uses chart analysis in combination with micro and macro considerations, previously identified trends and patterns, overall market sentiment and professional opinions to make an educated guess about what a stock is likely to do in the near term, generally within a six week to six month window. Once you get comfortable with the basics of buying, selling and trading stocks, it may be advantageous to check out other, more advanced publications on this subject in order to further advance your financial knowledge. In fact, I not only recommend it, I consider it essential to your future growth as an investor so that you can maximize your performance and make sure that the returns on your investments reach their full potential.

Disclaimer

Sic Figs encourages the reader to research and confirm the information and opinions expressed in this book to the reader's own personal satisfaction before acting upon any of the suggestions provided in this guide. You should give serious consideration to the suitability of any information or stock strategies provided in these pages and compare them to your own personal investment needs, goals and aspirations. Investing in the stock market involves risk, including the potential loss of principal. In fact, I can guarantee that **You Are Going To Lose Money!** Eventually. The goal of investing is to win more trades than you lose, stack your winners one upon the other and minimize the damage when you are wrong. You should always be paying attention to your own portfolio and the factors that may move it in one direction or another. You, and you alone, are responsible for your own money and the decisions that you make with your investments. Sic Figs is not a fiduciary or a money management entity and is in no way responsible for your success and failures.

CHAPTER 5: ALL ABOUT THE MONEY

Before we get started with the specifics, let's get comfortable defining exactly what it means to be "rich" and identify the end goal of what we're trying to accomplish here with the help of the stock market. According to the latest research and surveys conducted by the financial services company known as Charles Schwab, to be considered "rich" in today's American culture you generally need to have a net asset worth of at least $2.5 million dollars. Although, in some major cities the threshold is even higher than that, with San Francisco leading the way at $5.1 million dollars. It also differs by generation, with Boomers believing that "rich" is defined by having net assets of $2.8 million dollars, while millennials peg that number at $2.2 million and Gen X say that it takes an unrealistic (and stuck in the '80's) $1.2 million to hit that threshold. But no matter who you side with, they all tend to agree in principle that it no longer cuts it to just be a millionaire. Being a millionaire no longer makes you "rich" in the United States of America. And it hasn't for a long time. Aside from that, Americans said that it takes an average of $778,000 in net assets to live a financially comfortable lifestyle.

Statistically speaking, only about 2% of the population of the United States qualifies as being rich. The top 2% of households in the United States have a minimum net worth of at least $2.7 million dollars, according to Kiplinger. The top 5% is populated by individuals with at least $1.17 million. To make it into the top 10%, you need a net worth of $970,900, while cracking the top 50% requires $585,000. And in case you're wondering, to climb into that rarified air of being a one percenter you would need about $13.7 million dollars. But that only gets you in on the ground floor. To qualify as "super rich," you need net assets of at least $30 million dollars! So, that answers that question, but what constitutes one's "net asset worth?"

Net worth is defined as the value of all assets owned by a company, household or individual, minus the total accumulation of debt and liabilities. An asset can be defined as anything holding a monetary value, such as cash and cash equivalents like stocks and bonds, real estate: owning homes or land, jewelry, collectibles such as art, sculptures, cars (not the one that you drive every day-or you wouldn't be reading this), comic books, stamps, ect. Retirement accounts such as the 401K and the IRA also count in determining net worth (although I have seen some disagreement on this). Of the 22 million millionaires living in the U.S in 2024 (6.6% of the U.S. population), a record 497,000 were 401K millionaires in 2024, according to Fidelity Investments. An additional 398,594 IRAs held one million dollars in balance, accounting for about 4.1% of the total.

Now let's look at some of the reasons why you're not already rich and why you're not going to get there without the help of the stock market. According to recent data provided by the consulting firm Motio Research, the median U.S. family income for 2024 was $78,171/year. The most recent average savings rate for a family living in the United States is 3.4% (a decrease of 1.1% from last year). That means that the average family is saving about $2,657.81 per year. At that rate, it would take that average family more than 500 years to become rich by saving alone, and that assumes that the benchmark of $2.5M remains stagnant. Which it won't, since the benchmark was $2.2 million just a year ago. When you consider income distribution, it becomes even less likely that you will get rich through savings alone, as the income range for those Americans occupying the largest percentage of households at 16.8% falls into the range of $50,000 to $74,999. Education level, demand for your particular occupation and skill set and where you live will all play a role in dictating how much money that you have to work with. The average male earned a median income of $63,804 in 2024, according to the U.S Bureau of Labor, while the median female salary was a less impressive $52,884. Male residents of Washington D.C. had the highest salaries at $104,120, while Mississippi is this year's King of the have-nots, dethroning Arkansas with a median male salary of only $37,500. When you consider these numbers it is clear to see that you aren't going to get rich any time soon by working for a paycheck and saving 3.4% of what you make. Unless you're Moses, and plan on living for 900 years, it just isn't going to happen. If you are going to remember anything about all of those numbers that I just threw at you, the key takeaway is this: **your money needs to be making you money.**

CHAPTER 6: I OWE, I OWE (A WORD ABOUT DEBT)

Very simply, debt is something that you accumulate when you borrow money to pay for or finance something that you probably otherwise couldn't afford to buy outright. Most people (even rich people) need to take on some level of debt in order to satisfy their wants and/or needs and desires. That is normal. For example, if you've ever purchased a house or bought a new car, then you have most likely taken on debt to help pay for those high ticket items. What is not normal in the optimal sense is taking on a level of debt that exceeds your ability to pay it back, or otherwise cripples your ability to meet your other obligations, which may include saving or planning for a financially stable future. It therefore becomes important to be able to understand and differentiate between good debt and bad debt. An example of good debt is a loan that is used to finance something that will generate a positive return on the investment, such as the mortgage used to pay for a home, the hope being that by the time you pay it off, the house will be worth more than you paid for it originally.

Bad debt is sometimes easy to recognize and sometimes not. **Auto loans** are an example of bad debt because the commodity that you used the borrowed money for immediately begins to depreciate in value. It doesn't matter that most people in the United States need to drive to account for commuting to and from work. Borrowing money to lose money is not a good "investment."

If you are one of the many who must borrow money in order to purchase a vehicle, here are a few tips to keep in mind when purchasing your next vehicle. First of all, it is best to try and wait for a dealer or manufacturer's promotional offer, generally a limited time incentive offering a low-percent interest rate hovering around 0-2%.

Consider that even if you have enough money to buy the vehicle outright, it still may be more profitable to take advantage of a zero percent or low rate loan to make the necessary purchase. For instance, say you can finance the purchase of a new car for a special low interest rate in the neighborhood of said 0-2%. The money that you would have otherwise spent on purchasing that vehicle outright can then be used to make you money by investing it instead, either in stocks, bonds or higher interest certificates of deposit (CDs). In this example, the money that you would have spent on a depreciating commodity will be making you money instead, if you can just earn the average 8-10% on it that the S&P 500 generally returns per year or by parking it in a CD or savings account making a few percentage points more than the auto loan that you used to finance the purchase.

If you are planning on buying a new car, here are a few more things to keep in mind. The first is that what time of the year that you buy the car will matter, with the deepest discounts typically coming in December, with an average discount of 7.7% off the MSRP, according to Money magazine. Times of slower foot traffic can also yield better results, such as cold and/or snowy days, waiting until the end of the month or shopping at the end of the day. Always know your price when you enter the dealership and be willing to walk if they don't agree to meet it. Visit the Kelly Blue Book Price Advisor to identify the "Fair Purchase Price" of the vehicle that you are interested in, so that you can determine what you should be paying. Shop at least three different dealers, and when you decide where you want to make that purchase from, let the salesperson know that this other dealer is willing to meet your price (whether it's true or not), but you want to give him or her the business instead, if they agree to meet your price. I've had people with inside knowledge of the industry tell me that the sale price of a vehicle is less important to the dealer than all of the add-ons that come after, like service, extended warranties, special coating and rust protection, ect. Just say no to that stuff. It's just a money grab.

Perhaps the most notorious example of bad credit on this list and the one most likely to negatively impact your financial well-being, just for the commonality of its influence on personal wealth and the ease with which it can get the consumer into trouble, is **credit card debt.**

Credit card debt is considered bad debt for two main reasons in particular. 1) They come with high interest rates. And 2) The low accompanying payments combined with the easy access to credit and borrowing on impulse can result in the accumulation of sizable debt being serviced by those previously mentioned high interest rates. In the second quarter of 2023, credit card debt in the United States reached an all-time high of one-trillion dollars, for the first time ever. The average credit card user carried a personal balance of $8,674 (up from $5,733. a year ago) while paying an additional 20.53% interest to carry that debt. That's just OUCH! You cannot and you will not get rich consistently paying twenty-plus percent more on everything that you buy. That just doesn't work. In fact, if you are carrying any credit card debt at all that is rolling over month to month, then you should absolutely pay that off first, before you sink a single dollar into the stock market. Otherwise, you will find that the twenty percent that you're paying out to service your debt will completely swallow any gains that you are making in the market. Having said that, credit cards can be a useful financial tool when used responsibly and can even add value to your extended portfolio through cash back incentives and other rewards programs that offer discounts for certain goods and services. To reap the benefits of these and similar programs **YOU MUST pay off the balance**

of your charges every single month so that you carry a zero balance at the beginning of each payment cycle. Credit cards are also useful when you pay your balance off every month because unlike cash, most credit cards offer fraud protection on the goods and services that you buy and using them is an easy way to itemize and track your purchases. As such, they offer a level of accountability, security and traceability that cash just doesn't have.

Payday Loans. If you're using payday loans then you definitely ain't rich, and you won't be getting rich any time soon taking advantage of these weapons of mass financial destruction. Things happen and you need money fast. Okay, got it. Not everyone has the ability to pay for a sudden or unexpected emergency. But at the same time, payday loans are a real robbing Peter to pay Paul kind of set up. Except, you're really just stealing from your future self by borrowing against your next paycheck and shrinking it in advance by the size of the loan and the attached interest and fees. By definition, a payday loan is a short-term unsecured loan generally characterized by high interest rates, usually in the amount of $500 or less which is to be repaid on receipt of the borrower's next paycheck. Some lenders may require a verification of employment or income, such as pay stubs, others do not. Many do not run credit checks on the potential borrowers, but laws and regulations can vary from state to state and amongst the lenders themselves. The way it works is this: a borrower visits a payday lending store and secures a small loan, to be repaid off of the next paycheck that the borrower receives. The borrower will then write out a post-dated check to cover the amount of the loan and attached fees. The borrower is then obligated to return when they receive their next paycheck to repay the loan. If they do not return, the lender cashes the check. If there are insufficient funds to cash the check, then additional fees and penalties will apply. So, why are payday loans so bad? How about the 400% annual percentage rate that they come with, not to mention that these lending stores are usually set in lower income neighborhoods, which invariably end up taking advantage of those individuals most likely to need the service, but least likely to be able to afford it. The loans are typically structured at $15 per $100 borrowed, but other fees may apply if the loan becomes delinquent. Like the other forms of debt that we've covered so far, payday loans can be a useful tool in a pinch if used only with necessity and with the caution of paying off the debt when it come due, but unlike auto loans and credit cards, there is no real positive spin that you can put on using them, such as a cash back incentive, other than to bail you out of a temporary crisis. Relying too heavily on this form of borrowing may be symbolic of poor money management and will keep you in the poor house indefinitely.

Lending Money. Not really a form of debt, but it might as well be for the damage that it will do to your portfolio. As far as this book is concerned, this is THE cardinal sin of money management, since it violates the first rule of getting rich through investing. **Your money needs to be making you money.** And if you have handed that money off to someone else, then guess what? **It is not making you money!** For starters, research conducted on the practice of the lending of money between two people who know each other suggest that you stand only a 15% chance of ever getting that money back, doesn't matter whether you loaned that money out of good faith or have an agreement to be repaid with interest. You might as well have just kissed that money goodbye forever. It is natural to feel pressured or obligated to lend money to a friend or family member who has come to you in a moment of need, but **Don't!** Sic Fig's money management philosophy is based on a strict, clear and well-defined policy regarding the personal lending of money: **No money, Nobody, No Reason.** And here's why. The money that you have made for yourself is a measure of what your time is worth. It is the physical manifestation of the time, labor and efforts that you have put forth to earn it. By giving it away (either straight up or by lending it out and never getting it back) you devalue what your time and effort were worth in regards to making it. And that's just not okay if you're trying to get rich through investing. Think about it like this: if you worked a forty hour week and brought home $500, and then lent that sum of money to a sibling or a buddy to cover some "emergency" that is not your problem, and they never pay it back, you essentially just worked that week for FREE! Ask yourself this question: would you have otherwise just completed that 40 hour work week if you knew that you weren't going to get paid for it? Are you okay with doing 40 hours of volunteer work instead of getting paid? Because you just ended up in the same place. It is important to understand that Goodwill does not buy you entry into the land of the 2%.

Your time has a monetary value attached to it, and you should be using it to make yourself richer. Plus, when you lend money to an individual who is not managing their own finances properly, you end up enabling those bad habits and make it more likely that the situation will not correct itself, and it may even keep costing you money in the long run, since the borrower is likely to keep going back to the well until the spigot is shut off. If you want to be rich, then **Do Not** be your own personal branch of the local bank. It's bad for your own personal financial aspirations and it's just really poor money management.

Lastly, lending money to friends and family is an excellent way to destroy a relationship, especially when you consider that you are highly unlikely to get that money back. I've experienced this first hand. Back in the 90's, when I was still poor and a sucker to boot, I "loaned " close to $7,000 over a three year period to my ne'er do well younger brother, on my $8/hour salary and while I was a college student! He never paid a penny of that money back, and that resentment became the impetus for us eventually never speaking again. And that leads me to my final point: **never co-sign a loan for someone else,** or put someone else in a position where they can adversely affect your credit. People who borrow money against your name have no "skin" in the game and no motivation beyond integrity to pay it back. Again, **You Are Not A Bank!**After you are already rich and have achieved everything financially that you want to achieve, if you still want to give your money away for nothing, then that's your prerogative. Once you're rich, you've earned the freedom, the power and the flexibility to be generous. But if you're not rich and you want to be, then you need to be more diligent about what you do with your money. Never let anyone else dictate your financial success and failures. Lots of people will help you stay poor, but only one person can make you rich, and that's you. So take care of your own financial interests first.

Charitable Giving

Since we're already talking about giving away money, let's spend a few moments discussing the particulars of charitable donations and how you can use them to make yourself even more wealthy at the end of the day. Sure, giving to charities is a nice way to give something back to the community in which you live and work and do some real good in the world. But this is a book about getting rich. For the purposes of this discussion, we're going to focus on the ways in which giving to charitable organizations can reduce the amount of money that you're going to end up owing in taxes.

The primary financial benefit to giving a charitable donation is that doing so can be used to reduce your income tax, capital gains taxes, estate and gift taxes. In fact, itemizers can deduct anywhere between 20-60% of their Adjusted Gross Income (AGI) by donating to charitable causes, the exact percentage is dependent upon the specific qualified contribution made as well as the type of charity and the organization to which the gift was made. You can also use charitable contributions to reduce your capital gains liability by donating long-term appreciated assets. You are then able to deduct the fair market value of the donation from your income taxes. Charitable deductions can also be used to reduce the gross total value of an estate. Any assets that you give to charity can be excluded from the taxable estate as long as the recipient is a qualified 501(3)c organization. Annual income tax deduction limits are set at 60% of AGI for cash contributions and

30% for non-cash assets. Sic Figs suggests that you meet with a qualified tax professional to figure out which set of circumstances best fits in with your own personal financial or tax needs. Here are some things to consider before parting with your money: I'm not going to name any names because I don't wanna get sued, but there are some high profile charities that have been caught red-handed with their hand in the cookie jar, sometimes more than once. Similar to some less than Holy religious organizations, there are charities out there that hide behind the veneer of the public perception that they're doing something for the greater good to swindle the good hearted, generous and ultimately the gullible into parting ways with their hard-earned cash. You want to begin by selecting the subject of philanthropy that piques your interest, and then do your due diligence on the organizations that support that cause. You can begin with just a cursory check on the internet. If the organization that you're looking at has been up to no good, you'll most likely be able to see something about it on the internet. When selecting a charitable organization, give preference to registered 501(c)3 charities. This is a designation given out by the IRS and it means that the charity is organized and operated exclusively for exempt purposes where none of its earnings may be distributed to any private shareholder or individual. You will want to make sure that the charity that you choose will provide a tax receipt for your donation. Legitimate charities will have an Employer Identification Number (EIN) and they should be able to provide that number upon request. A failure to divulge that information is a lack of transparency and may be viewed as an attempt to cover something up. Charities are required to register with the IRS on an annual basis, as well as other state governments. If a charity has not done so, then those donations will not be tax deductible. Before giving to a specific organization, you should find out how much of the money that is collected actually goes towards helping the represented cause. They should be able to tell you that. Legitimate charities will have the option of accepting contributions through checks and credit cards (which are more readily traceable). Cash, gift cards and wire transfers are a bad sign if these are the only methods of payment that are accepted, since these donations are nearly impossible to trace. Avoid cold calls to your phone and street solicitations, especially following a natural disaster, as these are common scams. Any legitimate charity should be able to tell you exactly what they're doing with your money, how much is used to cover administrative costs and advertising, and how much goes to helping the cause that they represent.

CHAPTER 7: DEFINING THE BASICS: GETTING TO KNOW YOUR WAY AROUND SOME COMMON TERMS

Stock Market- Let's start with the basics. The stock market is the primary venue where investing and the buying and selling of publicly traded assets takes place. Investment assets can be shares of publicly traded companies, mutual funds, index funds, bonds and commodities. Trading takes place M-F (excluding federal holidays) from the opening bell at 09:30 am until the closing bell at 4:00 pm EST. The pre-market begins trading at 04:00 am and the post runs until 8:00 pm. Although anyone can trade in the pre and post market timeframe, it is usually limited to institutional and high net-worth investors. Your brokerage house may limit your ability to do so.

New York Stock Exchange- This is the largest securities based stock exchange in the world, based on the market capitalization of all of its listed securities. It was established in 1792 and is located on Wall Street in New York City.

Nasdaq- The Nasdaq is the second largest stock exchange by market capitalization on traded shares in the U.S., but it is the most traded venue by volume. The Nasdaq Composite is the index that measures the performance of the more than 3000 companies that trade on the Nasdaq and is known for tracking a large percentage of publicly traded tech-related companies.

Wall Street- This is a specific street in downtown Manhattan that serves as the epicenter for the world's largest and most powerful financial institutions, such as the New York Stock Exchange. It is the trading hub for the world's largest economy. It is sometimes used as a colloquial term to reference the stock market in general and the people who work there.

Market Indexes- An index that measures the performance of a particular sector of the stock market. It is an indicator of that price at which a stock is currently trading and can be used to compare prices in order to quantify past and possible future stock performance. There are numerous indices that track the stock market. Of these, the **S&P 500** is considered the "benchmark." When you hear that "the market" is up 20% for the year, they are referring to the S&P 500. It is the benchmark by which the performance of money management is compared. If you fail to beat or at least match the performance of the S&P 500, then you have "underperformed." It measures the value of the 500 largest corporations by market capitalization listed on the New York Stock Exchange and Nasdaq.

The **Dow Jones** is perhaps the most well known of the stock market indices. It was founded in 1896 by Charles Dow and his partner Edward Jones. It is the second oldest stock market index, next to the Dow Jones Transportation Average. The Dow Jones tracks the value of 30 large, blue chip companies, which trade on the New York stock exchange and the Nasdaq. A blue-chip company is a nationally or internationally publicly traded company that is financially sound and has a long standing reputation for offering reputable brands and services that have operated profitably over the course of many years. The Dow Jones is considered to be a gauge of the broader U.S. economy. Sic Figs uses it favorably to get a feel for the overall market sentiment.

The **Russell 2000:** This index tracks the performance of 2000 of the smallest publicly traded companies in the U.S. These are the 2000 smallest companies by market capitalization housed within the Russell 3000 Index. Theoretically, the Russell 2000 is where you might find companies with the most promising growth potential.

The **Russell 3000:** Is the index that tracks 3000 of the largest publicly traded U.S. companies by market capitalization.

The **Dow Jones Transportation Average:** Once only made up of railway stocks, this index now tracks the performance of twenty large-cap, well known companies operating in the transportation sector. It is considered an early tell on how well the economy is doing since most retail merchandise is moved by truck and rail, as well as other economically sensitive goods, such as building materials. Bullish and bearish trends in the market can sometimes be predicted off patterns seen in this index first. It is the oldest continuously active index still in use.

The VIX- The CBOE Volatility Index is a real-time market index that tracks the level of fear in the market and can be used to assess the level of market volatility over the upcoming 30 days. The VIX rises when investors become fearful and drops when investors are bullish. It is possible to trade the VIX through the use of ETFs and other investment vehicles.

Market Capitalization- This is the value of a company that is publicly traded on the stock market. It is determined by multiplying the total number of shares by the current stock price. As of the second quarter of 2024, the largest company on earth by market capitalization with $3.44 trillion is the technology company Apple (AAPL), followed by Nvidia (NVDA) at $3.182T, Microsoft (MSFT) $3.098, Alphabet (GOOG) $2.049T and Amazon (AMZN) $1.873T. Take note that all of these are companies based in the United States. That is not a coincidence. That is an example of the same **Free Market Capitalism** that has come under so much fire in recent years, with even our own politicians constantly attacking the best, brightest, most innovative and successful companies with litigation and charges of operating a monopoly. There is a good reason why innovation never comes from China, Russia, Cuba, North Korea, Vietnam and the like. Are the people who live under those political restrictions less intelligent than the rest of the world? It is much more likely that it has something to do with **socialism** stomping out innovation and limiting opportunities. Take a lesson America. **Stop punishing individuals and companies for being successful!**

Stocks, Equities and Securities- Stocks are shares in the ownership of a company that entitles the holder to a claim on that company's earnings and assets. An equity is the same thing as a stock. Once upon a time, these were paper assets that you had to hold physically in a safe place, like a safety deposit box. Now ownership is tracked electronically, a technological advancement which has taken an expensive and complicated process and opened it up to the masses, where once it was primarily limited to the domain of the wealthy.

A security is a broad term used to define any type of investment that can be bought or sold, such as stocks, bonds, mutual funds and ETFs. It gets a bit more complicated than that, but a full review of securities and what they entail is superfluous overkill to the beginning investor.

Bonds and Treasuries- A bond is a loan that you make to a government or company, where they agree to pay you back the face value of that loan on a specific date, paying interest along the way, usually twice a year. Treasury Notes are a U.S. government debt security with a fixed interest rate and a maturity date ranging from two to ten years. Treasury bills have short-term maturities and pay interest at maturity. Treasury bonds have long maturities and pay interest every six months. Although bonds are generally considered a safe, low to no risk asset, they can dip in value during an extreme market meltdown, as seen in 2008 and the first quarter of 2009. You can also lose your money if the issuer cannot repay the loan. They are low risk/low reward investments. They generally return anywhere from 1.5 to 6% ROI, or about half the historical average of the S&P 500, at best.

Options- These are stock vehicles that give the investor the right, but not the obligation to purchase a given stock at an agreed upon price and on an agreed upon date. They come in two types: calls and puts. A call is an option which predicts that a given stock will rise in value over a set period of time defined in the contract. A put is a bet that the stock will drop in price. Options come with a "strike," which is the price at which the stock can be bought or sold. The closer an option gets to its expiration date, the less valuable it becomes. Sources disagree, but most suggest that about 35% of options expire "out of the money." When this happens, the investor is out the premium that it costs to purchase the contract. These are higher risk/higher reward investment vehicles. They are complex, complicated and best reserved for experienced investors. The benefit of trading options vs the individual stock is that you can make many times the return on the option than if you had just bought the stock outright. Sic Figs does not utilize options in its trading strategy and is not the best source of information regarding their use. If they interest you, it is highly recommended that you research the subject thoroughly using a qualified reference source and understand the material thoroughly before acting on it.

Mutual Funds- An actively managed fund which pools money from investors in order to purchase a portfolio of stocks, bonds and other money market investments. Mutual funds are diversified investment vehicles which house anywhere from 40 to over 100 stocks. Because of this, you are already diversified if you are in a mutual fund. They can be separated by category of concentration and sector of the market, as well as by risk tolerance. Management fees, expense ratios and/or commissions apply and affect overall performance. Fees vary, but can range from anywhere from a low of a few percent to more than 10%!

Because of this, and the fact that they are diversified products as structured, Sic Figs doesn't recommend owning more than one mutual fund offering a low management fee and paired with a history of good performance, Fidelity's Magellan and ContraFund are good examples of this. Mutual funds are typical of retirement and educational savings accounts and have a reputation for underperforming the S&P 500, especially in consideration of the applicable fees. Keep in mind that the larger a mutual fund is, the more difficult it becomes for that fund to find ways to invest new money. This can result in underperforming the market. If you buy a mutual fund outside of a structured benefit, like a 401K or a 529 ESA, minimum investment amounts of $500 to $5,000 may apply, with an average minimum of $2,500 to initiate a holding, although you can find funds that require no minimum.

Index Funds- These are loosely managed funds, similar to a mutual fund, that track a specific market index, like the S&P 500. They come with management fees that are typically just a fraction of a percent, vs mutual funds, whose fees can stretch out to double digits. They are designed to match the performance of the index that they follow. Over the last ten years, only 27% of mutual funds managed to beat the S&P 500, according to Fortune.Com. The advantage of the index fund is that it only seeks to match the performance of its index, not beat it, while collecting a much smaller management fee.

Exchange Traded Funds- Just like an index fund, an ETF is a basket of stocks that track a particular index. The main difference is that ETFs trade like stocks, meaning that you can buy and sell them at any point during the trading day as long as the market is open. Index fund transactions occur only once a day, after the market closes. They may also have lower investment minimums and are sometimes more tax efficient. The sale of an index fund can generate capital gains taxes that are then distributed and passed on to every investor holding shares in that fund, even if that investor didn't sell anything. According to NerdWallet, this is less likely to happen with an ETF.

Penny Stocks- These are common shares of small, publicly traded companies that are listed for less than a dollar. In the broader sense, the SEC defines it as shares of a small, public company that trade at $5 or less. Either way, they are very high risk/high reward holdings. Sic Figs recommends avoiding them all together, since a stock trading under $1 for three straight months is at risk of being delisted. If this happens, you will lose all of the money that you have in that stock if you don't sell it in time. Sometimes these companies engineer a "reverse split" to artificially inflate their share price, but this just calls off the dogs momentarily and can't be viewed as anything but a bad sign. When you get a reverse split, the company divides the number of shares by a predetermined amount that causes the share count in your portfolio to drop, while the share price rises. It does not affect the value of your holding, but your broker will probably hit you with a fee for managing the split. Penny stocks look enticing because they are cheap and you can load up on shares, but this is generally not good value for the investment since these companies usually have no competitive advantage, no earnings, poor debt to earnings ratios and sometimes aren't even real companies. In almost all cases, you are better off sticking with established companies with a strong track record of positive earnings, particularly those who are leaders in their industry and have a competitive advantage over their peers. Rolling the dice on these types of stocks is called "**speculation.**" Speculating in the market means that you are accepting high risk on an investment for the potential of a high reward. Sic Figs recommends limiting speculative holdings to 10-20% of your portfolio at max. Keep in mind that stock market pricing is a reflection of supply and demand. A low stock price is a show of low demand. Wall Street is populated with the smartest financial minds on earth. If they aren't buying stocks in those companies, there is most likely a good reason for that. Just stay away.

REIT- Real Estate Investment Trust is a company that owns and in most cases operates revenue producing real estate. REITs can own many types of commercial real estate, such as apartment buildings, retail and office space, hospitals, hotels and more. They are favored by investors for their reliable income streams and over-sized dividends, sometimes paid out monthly. REITs are required to pay out a minimum of 90% of their taxable income in the form of dividends distributed to their shareholders. REITs can be a good way to compound returns quickly due to their generous dividend structure, but they are not risk free and can have their stock value impacted by variations in interest rates. Stock performance may lag the overall market, even when accounting for the dividend payment. They offer little in the way of capital appreciation aside from the revenue stream derived from the dividend distribution. REITs can be a good alternative to owning property outright since you collect on a portion of the rent without any of the liabilities involved in owning actual real estate, such as renters who stop paying, incurring costs from maintenance or damage to buildings and property, taxes, insurance and other expenses like snow removal and landscaping.

Master Limited Partnership- An MLP is a publicly traded partnership that derives at least 90% of its income from minerals and natural resources. Similar to the REIT, MLPs distribute the majority of their cash flow to shareholders, which are called "unit holders" in an MLP. Also similar to the REIT, the appeal in owning them is the over-sized dividend payments and the reliable income stream that allows you to compound your gains more quickly. The dividend can be set to the DRIP option on your brokerage account, this dividend reinvestment plan results in more shares paying out more money with every distribution. It's also true that capital appreciation will underperform the overall market, but like the REIT, you primarily own these for the revenue stream. These partnerships do not pay taxes at the corporate level. Distributions from an MLP must therefore be filed on FORM K-1. This is much more complicated than Form 1099-DIV, something to consider if you prepare your own taxes or use an accountant, who will charge you more to fill out the form. MLPs are not corporations in the general sense but considered "pass-through entities." They are required to pass at least 90% of their income along to their unit holders or investors. These "partners" are then on the hook to pay the taxes due on these profits, but because these are partnerships and not corporations, depreciation and capital losses also get passed on to the investor and these can be used to reduce the tax obligation on the distributable income that the unit holder has received. Also lowering the tax obligation of the unit holder is the fact that MLPs receive special tax benefits, and because most master limited partnerships are housed within the oil and gas industry, they are subject to owning assets associated with high cost and depreciation. This means that the taxable income for MLP is already lower than what might be expected. As a limited partner, the investor needs to pay taxes on the MLPs taxable income, but because of those special tax benefits, along with write-offs related to cost and depreciation, the distributable cash flow that gets reported is less than the taxable income on which taxes must be paid by the investor. This means that the unit holder will end up paying taxes on only a portion of the distribution, which amounts to only 10 to 20%. The balance is treated as a "return of capital," and that portion is tax deferred. That return of capital will lower your cost basis with each distribution, and over time this will bring your cost basis to zero. When you sell the position, you will end up paying capital gains on that adjusted cost basis, and this is where you end up paying the balance of the taxes due on the initial 10 to 20%. This is why they are considered "tax deferred." However, if you never sell your position and it gets passed along as part of an estate, you will never have to pay the tax deferred portion of your distribution. This is because when you die, the cost basis is marked up to the current market value in an estate, wiping out the adjusted cost basis of the original unit holder, and resulting in the tax deferred obligation being removed from consideration in the eyes of the IRS.

Value Stocks vs Growth Stocks- Value stocks are shares of a company that are trading below what their fundamentals, earnings and potential suggests that it should be trading at. Growth stocks are shares of a company that have the potential to outperform the market based on their future prospects. Growth stocks are generally newer companies that haven't reached their full potential yet. They are inherently riskier than value stocks and therefore can be more volatile, especially in a market pullback. Value stocks usually offer dividends, while growth stocks prefer to utilize that cash for growth. If they do offer one at all, it is typically small and not very significant.

Long Position vs Short Position- A long position refers to stocks that you own where you make money when the price goes up. This is what most people refer to when they think of stock ownership. Short positions make money when the stock price drops. With a short position, your broker borrows shares from another account and sells them for you. When the price drops, you buy them back cheaper than you sold them for, return them to the account that they were borrowed from and keep the difference. If you borrow short and the price goes up, you then have to **cover the short**. Meaning you have to buy the stock back at any price and return them, since you are losing money with every tick higher in the stock price. With a long position, you can only lose the sum of your principal and whatever gains you may have had. With a short position you can lose a lot more than that, since you must return the borrowed shares and must do so at any price to avoid even larger losses. This is called a **Short Squeeze**, and it can spike the intraday price of a stock by double digits. Short selling is risky and Sic Figs doesn't use this financial strategy or recommend it.

Common Shares vs Preferred Shares- These are both shares of a company that trade on the stock market. The major difference is that common shares have voting rights and preferred shares do not. Preferred shares tend to be less volatile than common shares and are given preference in dividend payments, liquidation and bankruptcy proceedings. Companies like to issue preferred shares because they keep their debt to equity ratio lower than issuing bonds to raise capital, while ceding less control to shareholders.

Dividend- We've been mentioning this a lot, so let's go ahead and define it. A dividend is a sum of money that a company pays to its shareholders either as a cut of the profits or as a reward/bonus. They can be paid out directly into your brokerage account on a quarterly (more common) or monthly basis. Some companies may pay out their dividends by issuing shares instead of cash. Avoid these, since a company that is issuing shares this way is diluting their EPS (earnings per share), and this will affect the stock price by keeping an artificial cap on how high it can go.

Ex/date- This is the first day that a stock begins trading without consideration to the next dividend payment. You must buy the stock ahead of this date in order to receive the upcoming dividend. It is followed by a **Date of Record**, which is the day that you must be a shareholder to count in the next payment. The final date of interest is the **pay date**. This is the day that the funds will be transferred to your brokerage account.

Overweight Underweight and Equal Weight- These are ratings given to stocks by analysts which speak to how the stock is expected to perform relative to the overall market in the future. A stock that is listed as overweight is expected to outperform the market. A stock at equal weight is expected to match the market's performance and a stock listed as underweight is expected to underperform. The same analyst may upgrade, downgrade or maintain these ratings over the course of several quarters.

Buy, Sell and Hold- These are also ratings given to stocks by market analysts. Buy and sell are obvious. A Buy rating means that a given stock is expected to climb higher, a Sell rating is given to a stock whose value is expected to drop. A Hold rating is a market recommendation that is given to a stock where analysts are uncertain which direction the price action is heading.

Gold and Silver- Despite what you might have seen in advertisements, gold and silver are not particularly good investment vehicles by themselves. Stocks and bonds have both historically outperformed gold, with the S&P 500 returning 10.4% on average since 1970 (the year the U.S gold standard ended) vs 7.7% for gold. Over the last 100 years, stocks have outpaced gold by a ratio of 3:1. But that is not to say that gold and silver do not deserve a spot in your diversified portfolio. Gold is considered a safe-haven asset during market volatility and a hedge against inflation. Unlike the company in your stock portfolio that may lose its competitive edge over time, gold has a long and sustained history of holding its value as a precious and desired commodity that dates back thousands of years. Gold is viewed as a good "store of value," meaning that it maintains its worth without depreciating, like the dollar, which consistently loses its buying power over time to inflation. One of the pitfalls to owning physical gold is the costs incurred in storing it safely and insuring it against loss. You may also incur a premium of roughly 8% above the spot price to buy and sell the commodity. Luckily, there are many ways that you can get the gold exposure that your portfolio needs. In addition to owning physical gold, the metal can be owned through mutual funds and ETFs, like the GLD. The GLD is the stock market equivalent to owning real gold, with the stock price representing about 1/10th of the spot price of the metal. The same thing applies to silver, with the SLV being the ETF for that metal. Another way to get exposure to the metal is to own shares in the miners, such as the previously mentioned ABX. Sic Figs recommends that 5-10% of your portfolio be held in gold or silver.

Cryptocurrency- This is a tough one. I'm going to have to admit that I've never really understood it. Cryptocurrency first came on to my radar back in 2017 when a coworker told me that she knew someone who'd made $80K in three months by trading it. I had never heard of it and didn't know what she was talking about. And that's the problem. By the time that you start hearing about some new, hot investment, a large portion of the "easy money" has already been made. Cryptocurrency is a digital form of currency designed to work as a medium of exchange through a computer network. It comes in numerous forms, like Bitcoin, Dogecoin and Ethereum. There is no doubt that for many people, crypto has been an incredible investment opportunity. The problem is that anybody can come up with their own form of digital currency, and they have. Dogecoin for example started as a joke. Cryptocurrency is not backed or regulated by a government or bank, and because of this, its credibility has been called into question by some financial analysts who draw comparisons of the investment to be something akin to one giant Ponzi scheme. A Ponzi scheme is an investment that promises very high returns, but depends on the recruitment of new investors to fund those returns rather than actually earning any money through investing itself. The recent FTX scandal seemed to back this perception up. FTX was once the largest exchange for buying and selling cryptocurrencies, a NY Stock Exchange for digital currency. They were accused of using a Ponzi scheme to misappropriate investor money to illegally fund other special interests. FTX filed for bankruptcy on November 11, 2022 after a run of customer redemptions earlier that month forced the company to admit that they didn't have enough capital to meet the demand of the withdrawals. Sic Figs position is that digital currency is going to be the medium of exchange in the future. Paper money will most likely be replaced by a form of cryptocurrency at some point. The problem that I see in owning cryptocurrency as an investment is that I believe that the U.S. dollar will eventually go digital, and it will be backed by the central bank. This conversion of the dollar from paper money to a digital format will most likely crush the value of Bitcoin and other pretenders to the throne. The dollar is a measure of the strength of the GDP of the most powerful economy on earth. It is not subject to the whims and idiosyncrasies of a tradable market, like crypto is. Unlike crypto, the dollar is the world-wide standard unit of exchange.

Having said that, I acknowledge that crypto has made a

fortune for many people. It has its own tradable market, like stocks, bonds, commodities, collectibles and the like. The question that I would ask is have most of the millionaires already been made here? Has most of the easy money already been made? In every stock position, there is a moment where the easy money has been made and the risk increases significantly. This can be assessed by numerous standards of measure, like the price/earnings ratio and technical analysis. How do you determine this for crypto? There is no price-to-earnings ratio that you can compare with the overall market. As it stands, Cryptocurrencies are very high risk/very high reward investments that seem to best fit into the category of speculation. You are definitely not getting in on the bottom floor if you buy them now. The upside is questionable and fraught with risk, and the downside is everything that you own in it. That is not a good or particularly advantageous risk/reward ratio, it's more like gambling.

Despite everything that I just said, I think that every portfolio should hold 5-10% of its assets in crypto, and here's why. The U.S. government is in trouble. And that's not a political statement, that's just the facts. The U.S government owes $35 trillion dollars, vs a GDP of $28.63 trillion. That means that the government owes $6.37 trillion dollars more than the value of all of the goods and services that the country has to offer. In other words, the country owes way more money than its even worth. And the situation isn't likely to get better any time soon. Our political system is such that politicians essentially gain office by promising things that they have to raise taxes and borrow money to pay for. This ultimately accomplishes two things. It makes the general population poorer, and it also puts the country as a whole further and further into debt. If the government gets to a point where it can no longer pay the interest payments on its massive debt, then the dollar may become mostly worthless. If that happens, then it creates a scenario where people start using alternative forms of currency as a show of lack of confidence in the government, and that could and probably will be in the form of cryptocurrencies. If this happens, then certain digital currencies will become invaluable. Don't believe that this is likely to happen? It's already begun, as evidenced by the fact that no fewer than fifteen different countries are maneuvering to replace the once mighty dollar as the standard unit for trade and financial transactions. This is also an excellent example of why you need gold and/or silver in your portfolio. The primary advantage that precious metals have over paper currency is that they sustain and grow their buying power over time, where the dollar is in a near constant state of decline, thanks to inflation.

Real Estate- While we are talking about alternative forms of investing, I want to take a moment to mention real estate, which is defined as a piece of land and the development that sits on it. We previously mentioned some of the disadvantages of owning property in the section on REITs, but it should be considered that for most people, the biggest investment that they ever make is buying a home. Real Estate and retirement accounts make up the bulk of an individual's entire net worth. In fact, Andrew Carnegie once famously quipped that 90% of all millionaires are made courtesy of real estate, and there is some real truth to that. There are numerous advantages to owning property that are self-evident, such as the monthly dividends that it throws off in the form of rent. It allows you to build up equity that can then be used as a source of low-interest capital. And like precious metals, it can be used to store wealth, since even through periods of fluctuations on price and demand, people will always need a place to live, and that guarantees that there will always be a level of demand that is ultimately immune to the weakening purchasing power of the dollar. Wealth advisors generally recommend that 25-40% of a person's assets be invested in real estate.

Earnings Season- This is an exciting time for investors. This occurs every three months and it allows you as the investor to see exactly what is happening with the companies that you've invested your hard-earned cash with. Publicly traded companies are required to give an update every quarter regarding the particulars of how the business is doing. This includes earnings, revenue, guidance with regards to anticipated future performance, and updates pertaining to the business model. Earnings announcements are accompanied by a conference call which allows investors to delve into the fine details of the company's performance. Earning season kicks off in January, April, July and October. It then runs for about six weeks each time. Earnings season begins with the banking sector, which can then set the tone for the season. You will want to pay attention to the **Top** and **Bottom Line.** The top line is **earnings per share.** This is how much money a company made or lost per share. The **bottom line** is revenue. Both components will either **meet, beat or miss** analyst predictions for that quarter, and this will determine how the stock price reacts. Reactions are hard to predict. A top and bottom line beat with good guidance may drive the stock price up in a bullish market, but may be ignored in a market-wide sell off. A beat may also touch off a period of profit taking if that company's stock price ran up hard into the earnings report. A miss on the top and/or bottom might cause the stock price to drop, but it may go the other way if the miss wasn't as bad as expected or if it was accompanied by improved guidance. Sometimes, the conference call will cause a reversal of the initial response to the earnings report. Investors should consider waiting at least two or three days before reacting to a report.

Bull vs Bear- A **Bull Market** is a market where the price of stocks rises over an extended period of time, encouraging even more buying. A **Bull** in investing terms is someone in the stock market who buys and holds stocks, with the expectation that the price is going to increase within a relatively short period of time. A **Bear Market** is one in which stock prices continue to drop over an extended period of time. Bear markets officially occur when a broad market index falls at least 20% off the recent market highs. Conversely, bull markets happen when a broad market index climbs 20% from the market lows. A **Bear** in investing is a speculator in the stock market who believes that the prices are going to be going down in the short-term.

Stock Market Correction- This is a pullback from the market highs, but not necessarily a reversal from a bull market to a bear market. A correction is a sustained pullback of more than 10% but less than 20%. Corrections are one of your best opportunities to make money in the stock market. They represent the chance to buy high quality stocks from your watchlist at a much lower price. A correction is not the same thing as a crash. A stock market crash is defined by rapid and sudden panic selling in response to some macro event, such as the Covid shutdown in 2020 or the banking crisis in 2008. It is more difficult to define a bottom or a buy point in stocks during a crash because the fundamentals won't matter and stocks will violate their chart trends due to the panic selling.

Stock Market Ticker and Ticker Symbol- A stock market ticker is a banner that streams across a screen, either on a television or computer, that provides up to the moment transaction and price data for securities trading on an exchange, such as the New York Stock Exchange and the Nasdaq. The price is continuously updated throughout the day. The **Ticker Symbol** is a unique series of letters assigned to a security for trading purposes.

Stock Broker- Just like you have a bank to handle all of your banking needs, such as savings and checking accounts, you need an on-line brokerage account to handle all of your trading needs. The two can be readily linked to facilitate moving transactions easily between each, like funding the brokerage account to get started and moving trading profits back to a savings or checking account. There are many on-line brokerage firms that you can choose from and there aren't that many differences between them. Most of them nowadays offer $0 commissions for on-line trading, although there are fees for things like trade assistance, reverse stock splits, trading options and the like. Selecting a broker usually comes down to how good the platform and trading tools are. Check on-line to find a brokerage service that best fits your needs.

Limit Order vs Market Order- These refer to the condition that you set for executing a trade. When you use a limit order, you are telling the broker to buy or sell a stock at a specific price, which it may or may not hit. If it doesn't hit your price, the trade will not be executed. A market order tells your broker to buy or sell at random, without regard to your best interest and at the mercy of the fluctuating price that is occurring at that moment at which you are trying to buy or sell. Always use limit orders to execute a trade. You don't want to give the broker permission to satisfy your order by trading on a random spot price. It could and probably will be much higher or lower than you wished for.

Stop Loss- This is a price limit at which you tell the broker to sell part or all of your position at some point in the future (within 3 months) should that stock fall to a certain price. It is best used to lock in profits in a given holding, or guard against a reversal or sudden drop, such as an earnings miss or broad market sell-off. This way, you are not subject to surrendering all of your gains in a downturn or market correction.

Sic Figs likes to employ rolling stop losses in its investment strategies from time to time. Here's how it works: say a position has climbed to double digit profits and is either approaching or climbing above its point of resistance, we may determine based on market sentiment to let it ride by setting a stop loss, minus 5-7% of the gain. The stop loss is then adjusted daily on each tick higher, so that a portion of the move is secured. If the price drops, then the stop loss is maintained at the last setting, until it eventually hits and executes the order. This guarantees that we don't give all of our unrealized profits back (unrealized profits are the gain that you have in a stock that you have not sold), money that would be lost if a stock continued to simply fall in price. The inherent problem here is that you will never capture the full amount of the move up by utilizing a rolling stop loss, but keep in mind that you shouldn't be trying to capture the top anyway, the goal is to consistently stack winners one upon the other and limit the downside. Even professional investors rarely capture the absolute top of a move higher, it's just plain luck if you happen to do so. Trying to time an exit for maximum profit can cause you to lose the moment altogether, and then hold on too long as you wait for another chance to sell that ultimately never comes. In the meantime, you've given away all the profit that you had.

The other thing to consider with stop losses is that the execution of market orders can cause your stop loss to hit, even if the price in the current trading market made you think that it was safe for further gains. That kind of unanticipated action might leave you disappointed that your position sold. Sic Figs recommends the use of rolling stop-losses in situations where you want to execute some firm discipline in a position where you have already made a significant profit and want to make sure that you don't end up giving it all back.

Stock Split- This happens when a company increases the total number of its outstanding shares in order to make the stock price more affordable for investors. For example, say that a particular stock is trading at $1,000/share and the company announces that they are going to execute a 10:1 stock split. The stock would then begin trading at $100/share on the given date. Your individual share count would increase ten-fold, although the value of that holding would not change, since the share price is now lower. The advantage for the company is that it makes the stock price more attractive to new investors, while the individual holder benefits from a new round of potential buying.

Cost Basis- This refers to the original price of a capital asset plus the cost associated with buying the asset. Capital gains and losses are computed by subtracting the cost basis from the value of the asset at the time that it is sold.

Long Term Capital Gains- This is the money that you made on assets that you held for more than one year. They are taxed at a lower rate of 0-20%, depending on your taxable income. The typical rate is 15%.

Short Term Capital Gains- This is money that you made on an asset held for less than one year. These are taxed as ordinary income, which is generally higher in most cases than the 15% rate for long term capital gains.

Day Trading- This refers to a trading strategy where an investor buys and sells stocks throughout the day, attempting to profit from small fluctuations in price. Day trading usually involves a margin account (money borrowed from the trader's broker) and is considered a higher risk strategy. Sic Figs does not day trade and does not recommend this strategy.

Securities and Exchange Commission- This is the government agency that regulates and makes rules for the stock market. They also police the market, investigate and punish companies and individuals accused of violating market rules. Their mission is to make investing in the stock market safer for the investor. Companies that come under scrutiny from the SEC for potentially fraudulent practices, such as accounting anomalies can drop double digits in a single trading session.

Compound Interest- You want to know how to get rich over time? This is it. Compound interest is interest that you earn on interest. The key here is that it compounds monthly and yearly, so you continuously get paid interest on ever increasing amounts, which means that every payment is larger than the one before. This is obviously less impressive with smaller numbers, but over time the numbers eventually begin to increase rapidly. It truly is one of the methods that the rich use to keep getting richer, and it can work for you as well. This is the reason why Sic Figs likes to compound monthly dividend gains from REITs by setting it to DRIP. The dividend gets paid out on an ever increasing share count, so that the deposit gets bigger every single month, even if the dividend rate remains unchanged.

CHAPTER 8: THE SIC FIGS METHOD OF INVESTING

Sic Figs' method for investing in the stock market is primarily based on identifying and taking advantage of repeating bankable trends, to stack gains one upon the other by using a combination of chart analysis, observation and up to date information to form a hypothesis about what a stock is likely to do in the short term. The key word here is **trends**. It is unnaturally surprising on the surface of it, just how often the market in general and specific stocks in particular are prone to following established patterns. But it happens, and it happens with a frequency that is probably due in part to the fact that the stock market is a human construct, and humans by nature are creatures of habit. So it makes sense when you think of it in those terms, and that sets up a scenario where you can take advantage of the patterns once you learn what to look for. Keep in mind that once you identify a repeating trend or pattern, you will necessarily then be able to identify optimal entry and exit points. **Don't get greedy!** Take what the market is giving you. Get in and get out with the money. Warren Buffet, investing superstar and currently the sixth richest person in the world, once compared getting rich to the growth of an oak tree. It takes time, "Someone is sitting beneath the shade today because someone planted a tree a long time ago," he said. Take your wins and stack them one upon the other, and understand that it is a lesson learned the hard way to find yourself in a hole that you can't climb out of because you took on too much risk. Buffet also famously said that his number one rule of investing is "Don't lose money." Disabuse yourself of that notion. It isn't going to happen. Everyone gets a move wrong once in a while, there are simply too many factors that can affect it, and not even preparation will prevent or exclude it from happening to you.

Before we start to delve into the specifics, there are a couple of less sexy things that you need to do before you start building out your portfolio that will put you in a better position to be more successful later on. 1) Identify which sources of information best fit your investment mood, and 2) Start putting a watchlist together.

Identify your Sources. What do I mean by this? Information will be your best friend as an investor, so you need to immerse yourself in reading up on the latest news and events as well as watching stock-related television programs with regularity, if not daily, to keep abreast of the latest micro and macro catalysts that are moving the market, individual stocks and influencing market sentiment. Some sources Sic Figs relies on are the CNBC network for shows like Squawk on the Street in the morning, The Halftime Report at noon. Fast Money after the closing bell and Mad Money with Jim Cramer in the evening. All of these programs are a good source of news, stock market analysis, pertinent information and inspiration. They are a rich source of ideas and data that you can use to make an informed decision about what to buy, what interests you, what to avoid and why. Consider visiting on-line investment sites like Yahoo Finance. From there, you can access a host of useful daily articles and news feeds from financial media websites such as Investopedia, Zachs and Motley Fool. There are monthly periodicals that you can probably peruse for free at your local library, like Smart Money, Money, Forbes and Kiplinger's. All of these and many others are an absolute goldmine of information that you can use to get a leg up in making money in the stock market. Find the ones that suit your fancy and use them to your advantage.

A word of advice, don't believe everything you read, see and hear! Confirm investing ideas by vetting them against multiple sources. There are more than a few quacks out there that want to prey on your financial naivety. One that drives me crazy is the radio ad that I've heard many times that promises 20% gains in the stock market with zero risk. This is an unmitigated pile of nonsense! You know who promises 20% and no risk? **Scammers.** That's who. Every person who has ever invested money extensively in the stock market has been wrong at least once, and that's a fact.

Another one that gets me is the ad that suggests that you move all of your retirement assets to gold, because gold has increased "this much" in the last 20 years. We've already covered the pros and cons of investing in precious metals, so we don't need to do it again. Suffice it to say that gold did enjoy a power move from 2001-2012, climbing from $270 at the start of the 2000s to over $1,600 per ounce by 2012. As it sits today (in 2024), gold is selling for $2,516.40 per ounce. That's an 831% gain in the last quarter century. Since 2000, gold has outperformed stocks. But it should be stated that these moves tend to be generational and are not indicative of long term success over many decades. Precious metals still underperform stocks historically and should be no more than 10% of any portfolio, or 20% at max. If it is more than that, then there is a good chance that you're underperforming the market, and that is not what you want from your retirement accounts.

Third, be aware that not every financial "expert" knows what the hell they're talking about. Case in point, there is a very popular investment and wealth building book that has spent time on the bestseller list that will do you more financial harm than good if you believe what it says, and if you read that book before you got your hands on this one, then you wouldn't know that much of what this popular author says is just plain stupid at best and downright terrible advice in its worse moments. I read his book on loan after an associate who knew that I was an avid investor praised its teachings to me. Needless to say, I was dumbstruck by what I read. It's not appropriate to reveal the name of the author that I'm talking about or mention the title of the book, but just be aware that Sic Figs is not alone in their criticism of this "investor" and his famous book. The takeaway here is that you should consider any and all investing tips, strategies and advice for suitability regarding your own investing needs, goals and aspirations by verifying information over the opinions of multiple sources. To be fair, this author is rich, and you can't argue with success. But it's also true that a large portion of his income comes from selling franchises to individuals who use the famous brand to host expensive investing seminars. That is what mid-level marketing schemes do, and that has nothing to do with investing.

Build Your Watchlist. Don't underestimate how important it is to build and maintain an up to date watchlist. It will be the key to your success going forward, your playbook of sorts. Like a writer with an outline, this is going to be your starting point for most of the decisions that you make. Your watchlist should be a compilation of up to 25 stocks that you put together that interest you, companies that you may be interested in trading if you get the right opportunity to do so, the top 5-7 of which you will know inside out. The list can be maintained on your broker site, Yahoo Finance or the stock app on your phone or computer, wherever you track the market from. It will be populated by companies, industries and sectors that you understand, patronize or have some kind of personal affinity for. **Always know what you are trading!** An effective watchlist will be accompanied by target buy and sell points for each stock, and some manner of notification for when your price point hits. Sic Figs recommends sticking predominately to high quality companies that have good earnings, are leaders in what they do and own some sort of competitive advantage. Only put money into investments that you clearly understand. Know exactly what the company does, how it makes its money, what its competitive advantages are and what might threaten that position, such as lifestyle changes, regulation, changes in the specific sector that might make what your company does become obsolete, ect. Your watchlist should have enough diversity in it to promote a well rounded portfolio.

Diversity. There are a few things to consider when building a portfolio, and foremost is diversity. The size of your portfolio will determine how many holdings you have, but generally speaking you should hold a minimum of 3 stocks and no more than 7. You don't want to amass your own mutual fund because the returns per holding will be too diluted. Sic Figs likes to move between 3 and 5 positions, with roughly ⅓ of the account in each flagship holding. You should always consider having some cash as one of your positions so that you have it available to you and ready to strike if an unexpected opportunity arises. Diversifying your portfolio means that the holdings are spread out amongst numerous different sectors and industries. This is important because the market regularly goes through sector rotations throughout the year, and you don't want to get caught being heavy in the sector that has gone out of favor.

There is also the danger of a single stock wiping you out. For example, back in 2013 Sic Figs went too heavy in Linn Energy (LINE). I was attracted to the 9% dividend and had made the risky decision to briefly put most of my portfolio in LINE in order to receive the fat dividend payment. I did this just as the SEC announced that they were investigating Linn over their accounting practices. In early July, my entire portfolio dropped over 30% on the news. It set me back 22% for the year and it took a whole year to make the money back. By contrast, the S&P 500 returned 32.3% in 2013 compared to my -22%. And it was all because I wasn't diversified. LINE eventually went bankrupt, so I'm lucky that I wasn't totally wiped out right then and there. A more extreme example of not having a diversified portfolio is the collapse of Enron in 2001. Enron had encouraged their employees to hold only company stock in their 401K accounts, and many of them complied. When the company went bankrupt in December of 2001 all of those accounts became worthless. That's why it is important to spread your assets around to distinctly different companies in unrelated sectors. Consider banking, tech, industrials, retail, consumer staples, healthcare, utilities, energy, real estate, financial services and information technologies. Decide where your interests lie when putting together your watchlist. Sic Figs likes to have a mix of two or three high quality stocks paired with one or two income positions and maybe a speculative holding. The speculative position is one that is high risk with the potential to return outsized gain. Examples of this historically have included small cap biotech and cannabis stocks, but this is subject to change and is not a recommendation.

Discipline. Sounds easy enough. But it isn't. Other than diversification, perhaps nothing will dictate your level of investing success more than discipline. It is exceedingly difficult to buy stocks when everyone else is panicking, and it is equally difficult to sell a stock that is flying high and making money every day. But you should be doing both of these things. To be successful, you need to have a game plan, you need to identify what you like and at what price ahead of time. You need to know what the buy price of a certain stock is and where it should be sold. And then stick to what your research has suggested will most likely happen. Without discipline, several emotionally charged tendencies will get in the way of your success. 1) You're afraid that you'll miss a move if you wait too long, so you buy too early. 2) You've hit your sell price but the stock keeps going up. You want every last penny so you overstay your welcome and now the stock is below your sell point. Now you won't sell it because you're just waiting for it to bounce one more time. And it doesn't. Back in 2011, I caught a short squeeze in my speculative position in China Marine Food Group (CMFO). In one afternoon, my position rose 30%. I was thrilled, but I figured that I would sell on the second wave of buying that never materialized. The next day it was down slightly, but now I wouldn't sell because I wanted to at least get the price that I could have gotten the day before. This mentality followed me all the way to the red, where I ended up selling it for a loss. The company eventually got delisted for failing to report its earnings, something that is always a terrible sign and should prompt you to sell immediately. 3) You buy something just because it's smoking hot. It's way off its buy point, it's probably way over its sell price, but you figure that you will just capture the few more points up that it has in it. And then you don't. You get those couple of points, but you just want a couple more. Without discipline, you are always going to want "a couple more points." And you will probably end up losing money instead. Stick to your watchlist and trust the numbers that your analysis has given you. Even if it hurts, and it will. But at least you won't lose money. Keep this in mind, one of the dumbest things that you can do in the stock market is to give back a huge gain. If you stick to your analysis, you won't.

CHAPTER 9:
CHART ANALYSIS
AND TRENDS

This is the meat and potatoes of Sic Figs' strategy for making money in the stock market. There are two main types of trends that we want to pay attention to. The first are broad market trends that have proven to be reliable over the course of several years to many decades. And the other are stock specific trends that can be gleaned either from chart analysis or noted through observation over a period of several quarters to a couple of years.

The most common broad market trend that you can put to good use is one that will tell you exactly when the best and worst times to be buying stocks are. In general, the most bullish time to be a buyer of stocks occurs during the first seven months of the year. The start of a new year creates optimism, and this combined with an infusion of money into the stock market from 401K and IRA contributions tends to make December and January both good bets for positive returns. This is referred to as the "January Effect." It is worth noting here that since WWII, the market has been positive for the year 85% of the time when January is an up month. Aside from that, April has been the best month for the Dow Jones going back to 1950, returning an average of 1.9%. But over the last 10 years, the best month has been July, returning an average of 3.3% on the S&P 500. This means that the popular saying "sell in May and go away" is just that, a popular saying. In reality, if you sold in May, you managed to miss out on the historical best month of the year! June however, is typically weak, making it the exception to the first seven month theory. Since 1928, September has had an average return of negative 1%, making it the worst month of the year for owning stocks. August and October are also bad, with October being the most volatile month for stocks since 1950, owning more 1% swings in the S&P 500 than any other month per LPL Financial. Also making October a daunting month is the fact that it marks the end of the year for hedge funds, who start liquidating their positions to meet redemptions. February can also be weak, as it runs into profit taking courtesy of the strength in January. Going back to October, once the selling exhausts itself, the buying typically resumes in November in anticipation of the "Santa Claus Rally" and the January Effect. The Santa Clause rally is a particularly strong week of trading that happens over the last five days of the year and the first two trading days of the new year. This phenomenon was observed 58 times in the S&P 500 between 1950 and 2022. Sic Figs' own track record favors January, with an average return of 5.4% for that month, followed closely behind by July with 5.3%. October has been our worst month, with a cumulative -4% return historically.

Another set of broad market trends can help you decide the best time of day to pull the trigger on a move. On days when the stock market is open for business, pre-market trading begins at 4am and runs until the opening bell rings at 09:30 am. All times mentioned are EST. This pre-market action is not necessarily indicative of how the trading day is going to play out, but it might give you a feel for where the sentiment is at least starting out from. Keep in mind that it is not unusual for key data points to get released at 08:30 am, like the jobs report or the CPI (consumer price index), this can shift momentum one way or the other and will carry through to the opening bell.

Once the market opens for trading, there are two trends that Sic Figs looks for when buying or selling stocks, and they happen at 09:45 and 10:10 am. The market (and individual stocks) will open for trading at 09:30 at a certain price, either up or down. The price action will then continue in that general direction, either up or down for several minutes, before it begins to reverse itself from the opening and head in the opposite direction, peaking opposite to the opening direction very close to 09:45 before resuming its original up or down trajectory. For example, your stock opens in the red (down). As 09:45 approaches, it will reverse its downward slope and begin to climb, it may even go green momentarily before resuming its price drop. Conversely, if your stock opens in the green, that opening price will get softer and softer as 09:45 approaches, it may even go red before it resumes climbing with strength. Why does this happen? Because there are plenty of hot hands who can't wait to trade and start buying and selling the moment the bell rings. There are also a plethora of queued preset orders that get filled once trading begins, all of which exaggerate the opening price, be it up or down. Once those moves exhaust themselves, you start to see the other side of the trade take over, briefly. For this reason, you should never trade anything immediately following the opening bell. You're probably conceding the best price if you do, and knowing that can help you time your trades better.

Keep in mind that throughout the day, there are numerous catalysts that can shift momentum in the stock market one way or the other. But having said that, 10:10 is a time to remember if you're trying to execute a trade. As in my previous example, you want to sell a position that opened in the green and then softened into 09:45. It then resumed climbing higher. With a degree of probability that is more likely than not, it probably came near its high for the day sometime between 10:10 and 10: 25 in the morning. Sometimes the strength will continue up to around 11:35 am, but if you sold your stocks in that timeframe sitting between 10:10 and 10:35 am, then you most likely captured the bulk of the points available on the move for that day. Take note that these are just trends. That doesn't mean that they happen every single time, because they don't, but knowing the pattern is something that you can use to try to maximize your best return.

Besides 09:45 and 10:10, the other time to concern yourself with is 1:00 pm. The immediate post lunch hours can give you the softest stock prices of the day and that's because hedge funds and other money managers tend to do their buying in the morning and their selling after lunch, making 1:00 to 3:00 in the afternoon a block of time best avoided for selling and profit taking. You almost certainly will not get the best price to sell in this particular window. Keep it in mind however if you are adding to a position or your portfolio in general. After that, the trading becomes a little more true to the actual sentiment until the market closes at 4 pm EST. The takeaway is this: in the absence of key data points or other information moving the market, your best time to execute a buy will probably fall between 10:10 in the morning and 12:25 in the afternoon, with a specific concentration between 10:10 and 10:25.

Now that we've nailed down the best months and the best times to trade, let's look at some stock specific trends that you can watch out for in order to maximize your gains. It is not unusual for individual stocks to adhere to bankable repeating patterns that show themselves over quarter to quarter or year to year. You just have to be paying close attention to your top five names to see these develop. One of the more common themes of repetition currently seen in the market over the course of the last several years is the trend for Apple Inc. (AAPL) to trade down after a product launch. This minor show of predictable weakness can provide a brief moment of opportunity to those looking to initiate a new position at a lower and better price than they otherwise may have gotten. Apple also goes soft every time the economic data coming out of Chine goes soft.

Other examples over the years have included Core Labs and Meta (the old Facebook). Core Labs (CLB) is a one time Sic Fig favorite that operates in the Energy sector and was predictable for its tendency to sell off after reporting quarterly earnings, no matter what they said. I figured out that if I bought CLB three weeks after earnings that I could ride it up into the next earnings report and then dump it right before it came out. With Facebook, I noticed over the period of several years that the price action always went soft in June, this weakness lingered into the July 4th holiday and then reversed. I identified July 7th from looking at its chart history as the day to make my move, assuming that it didn't fall on a weekend. If it did, then I bought the stock a day before or a day after the 7th, whichever was most convenient. From there, the stock would climb higher all the way into its late July earnings report, where I could usually sell it for a quick 5-10% gain, or wait to see what the earnings report brought. Sometimes it was safer just to take the money ahead of time, since a large run into an earnings report can prompt profit taking after the announcement, especially if the company doesn't shoot the lights out. Bear in mind that these are only examples of the kind of trends that you can find for yourself if you're paying attention. I do not recommend that you specifically trade CLB or META, as both of these stocks have been removed from the Sic Figs watchlist. Also keep in mind that trends will change over time and that these examples may no longer be following the stated patterns. Always take into account that the stock market is a dynamic and ever-changing entity, and you will need to keep up with the changes in order to be successful.

Chart analysis is where Sic Figs comes up with a game plan and defines the entry and exit level for each holding. If you want to get *really* technical about it, the analysis of a stock chart can be a very extensive, involved and deeply complex exercise, similar to problem solving in advanced mathematics. It involves the consideration of a plethora of trends and indicators that suggests what the market in general or a specific stock in particular is most likely to do. Some of the more common indicators that you will hear about include the famous **head and shoulders** pattern, which shows three peaks coming off a baseline, with the middle peak being the tallest (the head) and the adjacent lower peaks forming the shoulders. This pattern is indicative of a bullish to bearish turn in the price action. By contrast, the **reverse head and shoulders** is taken as a signal that a bearish stock is about to turn bullish. Also common is mention of the 50 and 200 day **Moving Average.** This is the average closing price of a stock taken over the given timeframe. Being above the 200 day MA tells traders to look for buying opportunities, while being below is an indicator to sell. The **stochastic oscillator** is an indicator that compares the specific closing price of an asset to its range of prices over time. It uses a scale of 0-100 where a score under 20 indicates an oversold market, and a score above 80 suggests that the market is overbought. **Bollinger Bands** are indicators that show the price range that a stock usually trades within. The **MACD** is an indicator that tracks changes in momentum. The RSI, or **Relative Strength Index** helps traders keep track of momentum, market conditions and warning signals for dangerous price movements. **Fibonacci Retracement** is an indicator that can pinpoint the degree to which a market will move against its current trend. These are just some of the more common indicators that you will hear mentioned as you pay closer and closer attention to the market. A deeper dive into the specifics of how they work and how to use them exceeds the purpose of this book, since Sic Figs only makes occasional use of the head and shoulders indicator and does not employ the use of any of the other indicators mentioned in their chart analysis and as such is not the best authority to be speaking about their efficacy. You can easily learn more about each one of these trading tools by using a simple internet search or better yet, by picking up an investment book dedicated to more advanced trading strategies than we pursue here.

Sic Figs chart strategy is focused upon the simple premise of identifying support and resistance, along with searching the graph between closing points on the chart that may be indicative of a repeating pattern. Let's take a moment here to discuss the anatomy of a general stock chart, seen below.

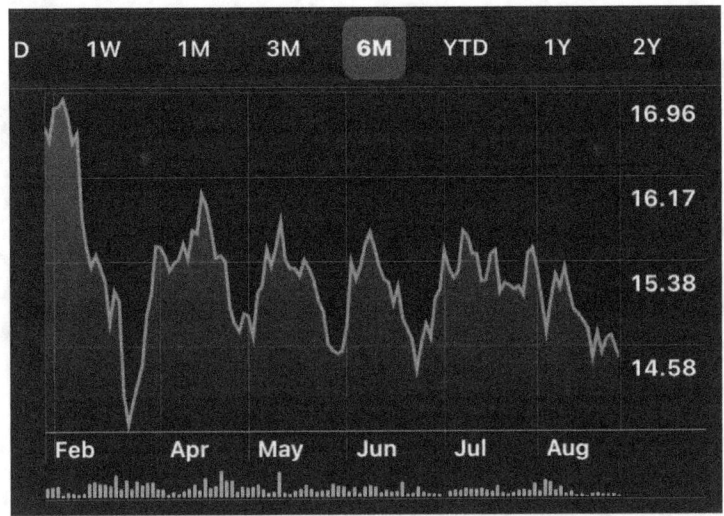

You will note that it is very similar to the basic math graph that you learned about in middle school, with an X-axis representing the passage of time and the Y-axis representing the price action. The jagged line moving left to right across the graph is formed by points representing the closing price for the given stock on a specific day. Stringing these points together forms the jagged line that you see. Note that the jagged line forms peaks and troughs as it moves left to right. Take note of the three peaks and troughs in the center of the graph. It is showing a pattern of lower lows and lower highs, which means the price action is bearish. Also note, and this is important, that you can draw a line along the bottom on these three troughs and it will correspond to a particular price on the y-axis represented on the far right. This is the line of support on which the stock will repeatedly bounce until the pattern breaks. Our buy price can then be determined by where the next trough will fall and bounce off of this line, and that is the point where the support line runs into the price on the y-axis.

In similar fashion, a line can be drawn across the peaks. This forms the line of resistance and while the pattern holds, the stock will hit this level and then refuse to go much higher. The resistance line will also correspond to a price on the y-axis as it runs left to right, and where these lines intersect will be identified as the sell point for this stock. This is how **support** and **resistance** is determined and this is where Sic Figs get their entry and exit points from. Be advised that as you determine your lines of support and resistance, that not every point will line up exactly. This doesn't matter. What you want to do is find as many matching points that you can and draw your line from there. You need a minimum of three points of agreement for the line to mean anything, but the more points that you have in forming your support and resistance lines, the more accurate the corresponding price will be.

Take note of the **flag pattern** formed by the price action as it is graphed along the chart. This is a technical indicator that Sic Figs does use and relies upon greatly. These patterns are money in the bank when you find them. In this particular example, 4 of the 5 peaks that we used to determine the line of resistance fell between the 8th and the 11th day of the month This means that if you were intending to sell the stock, you knew ahead of time that the best opportunity to do so would probably fall in this timeframe in a given month. Conversely, the troughs, or the low points represented by the line of support, repeatedly occurred very close to the 26th day of the month. If you paid attention to this pattern, then you knew exactly when the stock was going to bottom and when to buy it and then sell it for maximum profit (remember that patterns do break eventually). If you took the difference between the high of each peak and the low of each trough, you also knew that the average monthly return was between 7-9% consistently. Consider operating from the 6 month chart, as this will give you the best and most accurate information with regards to sustained price action, entry points and possible pattern formation in a steady market. The 1 and 2 year chart can be useful during an extreme market downturn to identify a stock's historical norms, while the 3 month chart can be useful in elucidating quick short-term trades. Now let's take a look at another example:

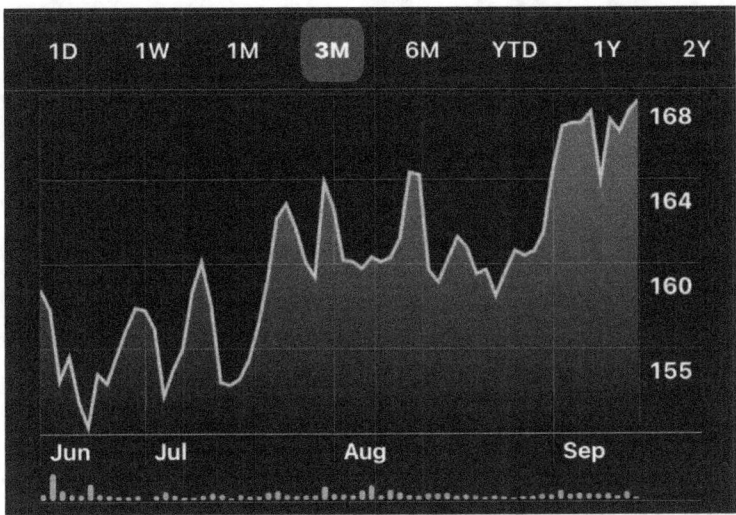

Take note of the peaks and troughs on this chart and notice that the price action has established a bullish pattern of higher highs and higher lows. In this case, there are four solid points of support that correspond to a buy price of $159.31 on the y-axis. Despite having eight distinct peaks, only about five are in rough alignment, beginning with the first point and moving right to the two peaks resting between the 1M and 3M marks, and then continuing over to two points corresponding to the 1Y mark. Unlike the support line, the line of resistance doesn't line up perfectly. That's alright. It doesn't have to be perfect, it just needs to be close enough to be accurate. Drawing a line across these five related points corresponds to a point that rests slightly above the top of our y-axis, which tops out at $168. By taking note of the scale between prices on the y-axis, we can extrapolate that distance with regards to that point at which our line of resistance would cross the y-axis, and that correlates to a sell price of approximately $170. The true top turned out to be $171.04 in this instance, before the company announced disappointing earnings and broke through its support line as a result.

Let's get back to bankable repeating patterns and talk about what else you can look for. Other than flag patterns, you may notice as you study a chart that you've seen a particular pattern before. You are not necessarily suffering from a case of deja vu. Sometimes moves on the chart will form a mirror image of a pattern that the price action formed previously, months earlier. This can be any shape formed by the graph over a period of trading days that forms a series of up and down moves, and then repeats those same moves in nearly the same proportions later on. Consider the following chart. This illustrates perfectly what a bankable repeating pattern looks like. In this particular instance, the move higher continued, topping out just above $17/share. It was money in the bank with very little risk if you saw it developing. But how would you know that it was going to repeat?

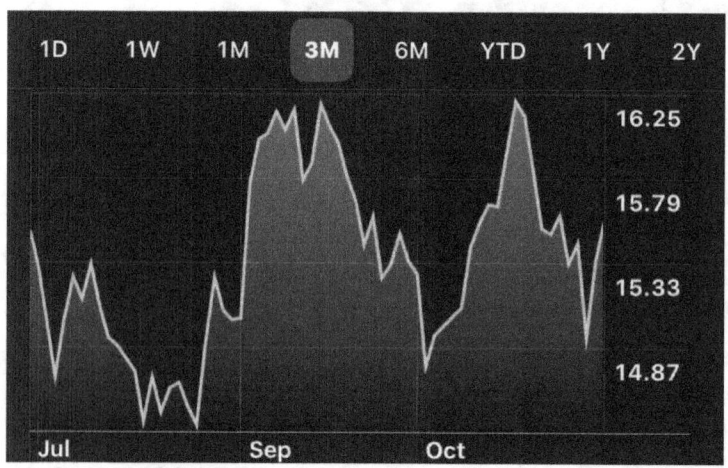

In this case, I would have been looking for a bump higher following the two consecutive moves lower, as shown by the chart action indicated beneath the YTD mark. This pattern mirrored the price action from one month earlier. Furthermore, if you plotted out the line of support, then you knew ahead of time that the move higher would begin around the $14.90 price mark, which it did. All that you needed to confirm the repeating pattern was to see it hold support and turn higher. KA-CHING$$$$!

Take note that this example was spaced out by a little more than one month's time, but they are most likely to be seen on the 6 and 12 month charts than the shorter ones because they usually need more time to develop. Once you identify a repeat move taking place, you can then use it to predict almost precisely what the stock is going to do next, as well as when that favorable price point is likely to occur. As previously mentioned, you can take the difference between a peak and a trough and then use that to predict the size of a pending move higher or lower, but you can also measure the distance between peaks and troughs and extrapolate that out to determine exactly when a stock's price action is going to reverse direction from bearish to bullish or vise versa. Sic Figs has successfully predicted changes in sentiment down to as few as two days by doing this. So I know that it works. Keep in mind that lines of support and lines of resistance are really just patterns at the end of the day, and patterns are subject to changing. Be prepared to change with them. In the example below, a previously bullish stock is seen breaking through its line of support after announcing an earnings miss.

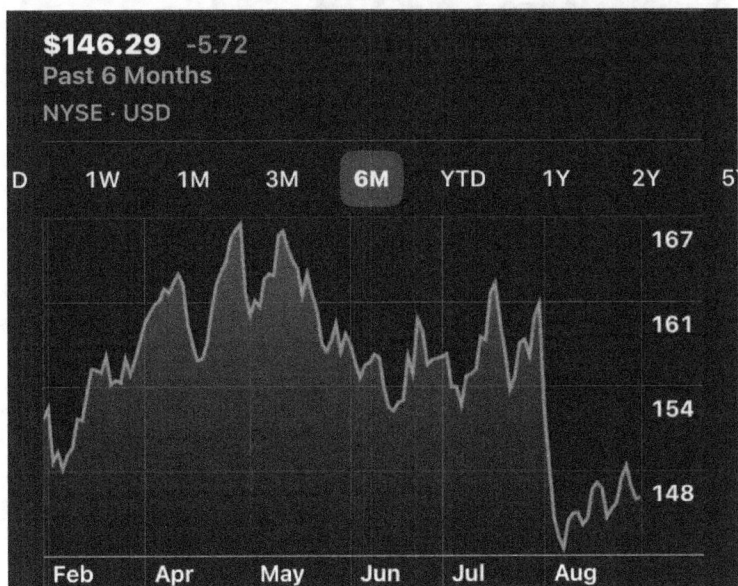

Note that even though it had held support on four separate occasions, it was also posting a series lower highs occurring at the same time that support was inching higher. This trend could be seen forming for three months prior to dropping below that support line. When you see a chart posting higher lows and lower highs, like this one did, it means that it's heading for an inflection point, or a change in direction. It is an indication that a strong move higher or lower is imminent. In my experience, these are almost always bearish indicators. Consider taking profit on any position where you see an inflection point forming.

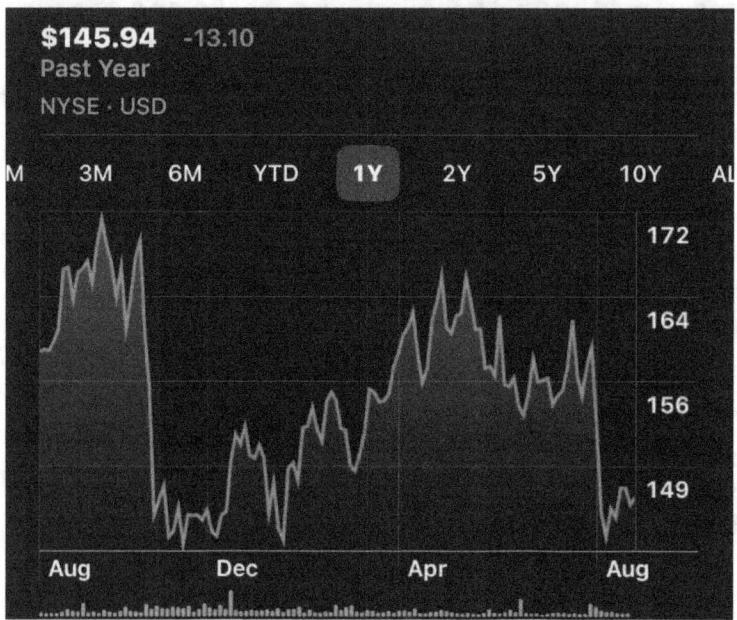

As you can see in the chart above, once the stock broke through support on the sixth month chart, the next level of support could be identified from the twelve month chart. In this particular instance, this stock also broke through the second line of support (seen below) after initially holding that 1 year line and bouncing. Once a stock breaks through two support levels, it should be sold without hesitation (if it hasn't been already).

As you can see on the 2 year chart, the main level of support is bearish, with the stock posting lower lows and lower highs over this timeframe, while hosting two bullish runs in between. The two-year chart indicates that this is a poor choice for a long-term holding. You could have made money during its two bull runs, but only if you had protected the bottom and sold resistance. Avoid stocks that have broken through support, especially on the one and two year charts.

Also take note that once a stock violates support, that line of support then becomes the new resistance level. As seen below:

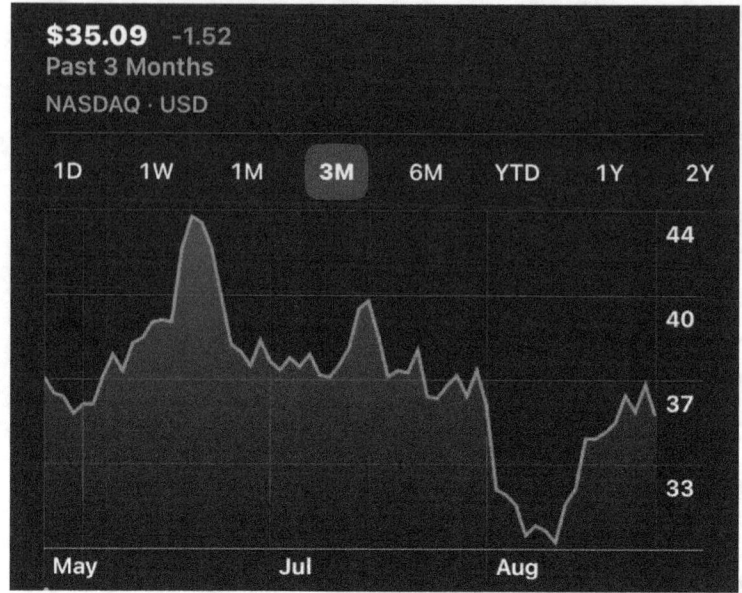

$35.09 -1.52
Past 3 Months
NASDAQ · USD

| 1D | 1W | 1M | 3M | 6M | YTD | 1Y | 2Y |

44

40

37

33

May   Jul   Aug

You do not want to have to break through two levels of resistance just to get back to even. The chart action tells you everything that you need to know about a stock's prospects for making money, but also consider that market sentiment had also changed regarding the company in this example, going from best in sector to second to its main competitor. That matters, and it was reflected in its chart performance. Always consider the technicals in combination with sentiment, timing, and macro and micro catalyst.

In the chart below, the indicated stock has the opposite problem. It has broken through resistance. It is exceedingly difficult to sell a winner that is climbing higher virtually every single day. But no stock climbs higher indefinitely. "What goes up, must come down," observed the seventeenth-century physicist and mathematician Sir Isaac Newton, and although he wasn't talking about the stock market, he might as well have been.

In cases like this where you have a high-flier that smashes through resistance, consider protecting your gains by installing a stop-loss at resistance. Then let the stock keep running, while you adjust your stop-loss with each point higher. In this particular example, the stock shown sits in the consumer retail sector, which is considered a "defensive" position. It is most likely going to get sold off hard on the next rotation to growth. During sector rotations, the money has to come from somewhere to feed the next hot buying opportunity. And that money comes from last season's winners. Sector rotations can happen three or four times a year, and this pretty much guarantees that your winner won't keep printing cash forever.

The key take away to all of the strategies that we've covered in this section is this:

1) Identify the support and resistance lines for each stock that you may be interested in buying or selling, and use those lines to define the entry and exit points on your watchlist.

2) Exercise discipline and stick with the information that

your research and chart analysis have given you. Don't panic out of a move just because some unrelated macro event is sending the whole market down and don't buy something way off your target price just because you're afraid to miss a move. It happens. Ideally, you would be buying into panic and selling euphoria.

3)   Don't nickel and dime it. You will in all likelihood not capture the absolute high or low in a given trade, and that's okay. You just want to be in the neighborhood. Sic Figs has missed more moves than we'd like to admit to by trying to time a trade to the exact penny. It's better to be in for 25 cents more than you wanted to pay for something than to miss the move entirely. This mistake has cost Sic Figs thousands of dollars in lost profits.

4)   Recognize that stocks have a comfort level that shows itself in patterns that repeat themselves. Review the charts and identify these opportunities when they happen.

5)   Be realistic about your expectations. Not every trade or investment will be a winner. The goal is to have more winners than losers, and stack those winners one upon the other so that over time you end up way ahead. In all likelihood, you are not Warren Buffett. There will be years when you lose money. You simply want to profit from your winners and then protect against the downside when you're wrong by knowing when to sell.

CHAPTER 10:
MANAGING BAD NEWS

You need to realize that sometimes events will occur that you have no way to predict and that no amount of research or chart study will help you see it coming. These are all scenarios where you should seriously consider just cutting your losses and walking away.

1) The dreaded **Accounting Irregularities.** I have already discussed how this happened once in the Sic Figs portfolio with Linn Energy back in 2013. The announcement set the portfolio back 30%, but the initial damage was only half of that number. The problem was that I didn't sell it right away. If I had, I might have limited the damage to only 10%, which would have allowed me to possibly break even for the year. Instead, I lost 22% on the year in which the S&P 500 was up over 32%. My cardinal sin was that I kept waiting for the stock to rally and recover some of the lost points, which it never did. It was a complete disaster, but not as bad as it could have been. LINE eventually went bankrupt and was delisted from the stock exchange. Sic Figs recommends taking the initial loss if this happens to a stock that you own, and getting out. Let the dust settle where it might without you. You can always get back in later if the company is cleared from wrongdoing and you really like the position.

2) **SEC Investigations.** You never want to hear that the company that you own stock in is being investigated by the Securities and Exchange commission. This can be the

result of something more benign to shareholders, like insider trading, or it can be something more serious like accounting inconsistencies, misinformation or omissions from earnings reports, not reporting earnings in the required timeframe, market manipulation and fraud. All of these are not good, but you may want to get a full understanding of the scope and consequences regarding what the company is being investigated for before you jump to sell.

3)   **Disasters.** The best example of this involves yet another company that Sic Figs held in one of its managed accounts. BP is an integrated oil and gas exploration company that saw its share price cut in half when the Deepwater Horizon drilling rig exploded on April 20th, 2010, killing 11 crewmen and the portfolios of everyone who owned it in the process. The event caused the stock price of BP to drop 54% over the next two months, and the costs associated with the cleanup and legal ramifications promised to hurt earnings for years. Sic Figs recommends selling company specific disasters straight off. You will probably lose more money by waiting for any kind of recovery. It is usually not worth it. Just cut bait and move on.

4)   **Earnings Season.** This is a tough one. Publicly traded companies are required to provide an update regarding their financial condition, including their earnings for the quarter, revenue, overall financial state, outlook and other pertinent information to shareholders and other potential investors every three months, plus an annual report. Ahead of these events, Wall Street analysts provide estimates for what they think these companies will say. When the earnings report is released, the company will meet, beat or miss on these estimates with regards to earnings, revenue and guidance. This determines how the stock of the company reacts. Sometimes a company reports a top and bottom line beat and the stock goes up. Sometimes they report an across the board beat and the stock goes down, because it ran hot going into earnings and the announcement prompted a round of profit

taking. Sometimes they report a miss and the stock goes up because it wasn't as bad as expected, or they raised guidance. And sometimes they miss on the top, the bottom or both and the stock gets clobbered. You never know how the market is going to react, but you should never make a decision to buy or sell a stock until after the conference call. Sometimes a stock will announce and then drop 3-5%, and then the conference call starts and suddenly it's up 5-10%. You need to play it by ear, just make certain that you don't overreact to the Street's first impression.

5) **Recalls and Litigation.** Again, this is not good, and it can hang over a company's balance sheet like a black cloud for many quarters to several years. But you should work to gain a clear understanding of the scope of the problem and the potential lingering ramifications of the outcome before submitting to a panic sell. Just know that the issue may suppress the stock performance and your portfolio as well. Sic Figs recommends moving off such positions. Why own a stock that has a built-in problem weighing on its earnings when there are numerous other places to stick your money without such worries? The answer is simple. You probably shouldn't.

Other Things Affecting Your Portfolio

1) **Strong Dollar.** The U.S Dollar Index measures the dollar's strength against a basket of foreign currencies. A strong dollar is a good thing if you happen to be a tourist, because that means you will get more buying power in a currency exchange. This is also a good thing for companies that rely on exports, but if the company in your portfolio relies on imports, then the difference in the conversion rate is going to reflect poorly in the earnings report.

2) **Rising Interest Rates.** The stock market loves the free money available in a low to no interest rate environment because it makes borrowing cheaper and it reduces the

competition between stocks and other investment vehicles. When interest rates are on the rise, the appeal of no-risk, higher interest treasuries pulls investment dollars out of the stock market, particularly income based holdings such as REITs, MLPs and high dividend energy and consumer staple stocks. When managing a portfolio in this kind of environment, it becomes even more important to keep the cost basis as low as possible by getting the best prices for the stocks that you buy. Because the margin for error is lower, you need to be more disciplined in your investing decisions to maximize returns.

3) **Inflation.** This one goes hand in hand with rising interest rates. Historically, inflation runs at a rate of about 2% a year. Any higher than that and it will pressure the Federal Reserve to raise the prime interest rate until inflation cools to the average. Raising the prime rate can have the effect of pulling investment dollars out of the stock market in favor of lower risk and suddenly higher interest rate options like CDs, bonds and treasuries.

4) **Consumer Price Index.** The CPI measures inflation. It tracks the variation in prices paid by the consumer for retail goods. The report is released at 08:30 in the morning, in the middle of the second week of each month, and can be a catalyst for sending stocks higher or lower depending upon the difference between the actual and the estimated number.

5) **Producer Price Index.** The PPI is a leading indicator of consumer price inflation. It is a collection of indexes that measure the average change in the selling prices of domestically produced goods and services. The PPI is published monthly by the Bureau of Labor Statistics and is released at 08:30 am EST on the second Thursday of each month. Many stock market analysts consider it to be more impactful than the CPI, with regards to inflation and its effect on market sentiment.

6) **Consumer Confidence Index.** Measures and compares how consumers view the overall economy, business conditions

and labor market. It provides insight into U.S. economic conditions, including the likelihood of consumers to make major purchases, such as homes and automobiles. It is released at 10 am EST on the last Tuesday of every month.

7)   **Non-Farm Payroll Report.** Released at 08:30 in the morning on the first Friday of every month by the Bureau of Labor Statistics, this report measures employment in the United States, and can also sway market sentiment upon its announcement. A weaker jobs report will spark fear that the overall economy is weakening. A strong jobs number will lend credence to the idea that the economy is thriving, and this may act as a short-term catalyst to drive stocks higher.

8)   **The Government.** Every four years or so, as election time approaches, politicians get together and decide that they need someone to blame for the mess that they themselves have had a hand in creating. Wall Street, as a symbol of wealth, power and corporate greed is a convenient target for much of this half-baked vitriol, as candidates take shots at Big Oil, the banks, Big Pharma and tech, weighing these companies down with needless regulation, restrictions and litigation, all in a barefaced attempt to fool the voting class into thinking that Joe Politician has their back. Of course, what these disingenuous jackass elected officials fail to consider is that Wall Street is not just a playground for the rich, it represents the hopes and dreams of every working-class slug who contributes to a 401K, IRA, 529, ect. Never mind all the mom and pop home investors out there that are just trying to stay ahead of the rising tide. So, what do you do when the company that you own in your portfolio comes under fire? Well, that depends. But the answer is, probably nothing. You will need to analyze each case on an individual basis, but more often than not it amounts to nothing more than a blip on the radar. Most of the time, these things have a predictable shelf life, and then the issue goes away. At least temporarily. Politicians are primarily just interested in telling voters what they think they want to hear, and making

promises that they either can't keep or have no intention of keeping. It has never really impacted any decision that I've ever made with regards to buying and selling stocks. Having said that, it is absolutely true that the threat of a government shutdown, arguments over raising the debt ceiling or a downgrade of sovereign debt can all put your portfolio in a world of hurt. Again, these tend to be ephemeral in nature and not a long term catalyst for worry.

9) **You!** I find virtually without fail that most of the time when I lose money, it is because I didn't follow my own investing rules. Sometimes, you just get blindsided by something that you can't see coming and have no way to predict. But most of the time, when I post losses it's because my discipline got in the way of my own greed. I chase, I overstay my welcome, I want just a few cents more. It really is way harder than this book makes it sound because you need to be rock solid about your discipline and commitment. If I religiously followed every single rule in this book, I would almost never have a loser in my portfolio. And that's the truth.

10) **Unrealistic Expectations.** Unless you win the lottery or come up with an idea that lots of people will want to give you their money for, then get used to the idea that you are not getting rich tomorrow. Building wealth is a process, and having unrealistic expectations will make you guilty of all kinds of things that will ultimately hamper you from getting there, like buying and selling with discipline and generally not following the rules and strategies laid out in this guide.

CHAPTER 11: MANAGING THE GOOD TIMES

Sounds like a high quality problem. And it is, but if you don't manage your wins properly you can end up giving back most or all of your profits. There may be no worse feeling in investing than knowing that you had a fat gain in your hot little hands and then let it slip through your fingers like sand on the beach just because you got too greedy. It happens. Just refer back to my previously mentioned story about China Marine Food Group. It is important to remember that even in the stock market, what goes up must come back down eventually. Whether it is courtesy of a short squeeze or a parabolic move up by a great company shooting the lights out on its earnings report, stocks will always revert to their mean either because the buyers get exhausted, the story changes, or they simply get thrown out with the bath water during a broad market sell-off. Disciplined investing means never giving back all of your unrealized gains. To ensure that this never happens, Sic Figs likes to employ a few different strategies to guard against it. The first thing to consider is, **always sell a short squeeze.** Every long loves a short squeeze, but by their very nature, the buying will exhaust itself and stock price will come crashing back to earth when it does. The problem inherent with short squeezes is that they happen because the short interest in the company is high, and that occurs because short investors think that the stock price is going to fall, usually because there is something about the company's earnings or fundamentals that is worrying. Any kind of good news will force the shorts to sell at any price, but once they do, the short squeeze is over and there is nothing to support that elevated price. This makes short squeezes an ephemeral event that needs to be taken advantage of as soon as they happen.

Similar to but not necessarily related, always consider **selling any large intraday gain of 20% or more.** Any move like this was most likely generated by news that caused a euphoric spat of buying by a group of undisciplined investors who are desperate to not get left behind. The problem is that this is the opposite of panic selling, and neither one is smart investing. If you are lucky enough to capture a big intraday move, then just take the money and run, or at least block the bottom with a rolling stop-loss. Sure, you're not going to get every last cent from the move if you sell, but you shouldn't be trying to do that anyway. You will never capture the very top or the absolute bottom when you're buying and selling, and trying to time your moves to perfection can cause you to miss the move altogether. You can always reset the position after the dust settles if you really like the company and want to be in it. The eventual profit taking will ensure that you get that chance. As for short squeezes, let it go. The move higher has already been made. Don't tempt your luck by resetting these positions. Remember that there are always one or two 7% + market corrections per year. Keep the price points updated on your watchlist, you will eventually get an opportunity to either initiate or reset a position at an advantageous price.

Aside from the occasional short squeeze and large intraday single event that sends your portfolio rocketing higher, the situations that you will probably have to manage most often involve moves where your position either chugs higher through a series of slow and steady gains until it reaches and then exceeds your resistance line, or sinks below your entry level price point and its accompanying line of support. Both of these situations require discipline to ensure that you protect yourself from loss, and both may benefit from the judicious use of the previously mentioned **stop-loss.** One of the main problems with consistently getting good returns on your investments is the temptation to put your discipline on the back burner for the sake of a few more dollars gained. It is really too easy to forget everything that you've ever learned about investing when you're printing money in a position virtually every single day, or slowly sinking in a move that didn't pan out. This is where the rolling stop-loss can be your salvation, since you set it without the emotion that will cut bait with your commitment to discipline the moment that it becomes inconvenient to your greed. The rolling stop-loss is based and set on the research that you conducted with your rational and reasonably functioning mind, before the move up or down started to mess with your thinking. Let's start with the easier one.

1) **Protecting against the Downside.** If you initiated a position at or near support, during a seasonally strong trading period of the year, then you shouldn't experience a problem. But if you find that the stock price falls after you buy it and closes more than a few cents below the line of support, then you may have a situation that needs to be managed. If a stock breaks support once, it probably isn't done going down. There are probably 2-4 more legs down until it reaches the next level of support, which can be many points lower. Sic Figs likes to block the downside in a holding by initiating a stop loss 5% below support. Doing this limits the loss potential. Sometimes it is better to admit that you got it wrong than to find yourself stuck down double-digits. It is easier to make back 5% than it is 10% or more. Remember, that if you lose 5%, you have to make 10% to get back to even. If you lose 10%, you now have to make 20% to get back to even, and that's just plain hard. This happens because after a loss, you are trying to make the money back by investing less in the position than you had before, because you lost some. Keep in mind that the stop loss is 5% below support, not 5% below the buy price, assuming that you paid slightly more than support to initiate the position. Also, I don't necessarily

roll the stop-loss when I'm simply protecting against the downside in a new and unproven position, although you certainly can roll it if that's your preference.

2) **Protecting the Profits.** In an ideal investing world, you would be selling resistance and banking the profits. But two things can scuttle this good intention. One is **greed**, and the other is **FOMO**. Let's talk about greed first. It is super easy to get complacent when the stock that you own climbs every single day right up to resistance and maybe beyond. Nobody wants to say "no thank you" to more money, but if you don't, this is probably what is going to happen: you're going to get enamored with the ever increasing number reflected in the account value of your portfolio and you're going to want "just a little more." The problem is that "just a little more" comes with an invisible infinity sign attached to it, because you ALWAYS want just a little more. And then the stock price drops and you get caught in the trap of only wanting what you could have had before, and this also self perpetuates as the price continues to fall. Pretty soon, you're taking a 5% gain just to save face when you could have taken 25% to the bank. It's just plain stupid. And yet so easy to do. Sic Figs manages these situations differently depending on the quality of the company, the strength of the overall market and the strength of the particular move higher. If all catalysts are favorable then the preference is to set a rolling stop-loss 5% below the closing price on a holding that has either hit or poked above resistance. I then increase that stop-loss on a daily basis to reflect the next gain. If the stock price drops, I do not reset the stop-loss. Eventually the stop-loss hits and you dump your position, but hopefully not until you've captured a few points higher than your initially intended exit price. If the market feels unfavorable to a move higher for any reason, I just take the money at resistance and call it a day. **FOMO** is just what you think it is. And yes, the fear of missing out is just another take on the management of greed. Because of this, it is subject to similar considerations. Ask

yourself this: What is the current market sentiment? Is this a high quality stock, a flier or a speculative position? Each situation may be handled differently to maximize the advantage. In a high quality company with good market vibes, I let it ride and protect the bottom 5% below resistance, and adjust it upwards with each tick higher. Speculative holdings are sold at resistance. No "if" "ands" or "buts." In a lower quality stock or in a market standing on shaky ground (maybe August is approaching), I just take the money and forgo the rolling stop-loss. The important thing to remember is that as you gain experience in the market, knowing how to best approach each individual move should become second nature to you.

CHAPTER 12: A WORD ABOUT RETIREMENT ACCOUNTS

A different type of investing than the ones we've been concentrating on so far, but no less important in your wealth building strategy, considering that after real estate, a person's retirement account is usually their second biggest asset. In fact, real estate and retirement accounts make up the predominant bulk of an individual's entire net worth. Having said that, about 50% of U.S. households (house of cards) do not have a single retirement account, according to usafacts.org. And 37% of retirees have no retirement savings whatsoever. Sorry, but that's not just not smart. If you're not planning for success, as the saying goes, then you've inadvertently planned on failing. Companies stopped taking care of their employees in retirement generations ago, and no one should be counting on a government that needs to constantly borrow money to pay its bills to pay for their retirement. Social security will not pay for all of your expenses in retirement, and it won't even be close, not to mention that social security may be insolvent by 2033 and Medicare by 2031. You also shouldn't be intending to work until the day that you die. For one thing, it's unrealistic to think that your health and body are going to allow that to happen, or that your employer will allow it. But whatever. This is a book about getting rich and you wouldn't be reading it if you were interested in being lumped in with that unenviable group. So let's hit it.

The absolute, hands down best advice that you will ever be given about saving for retirement is to **start early.** This gives you more years with the power of compounding interests behind you to make your fortune. Know that there are two main retirement vehicles available to investors: The company sponsored 401K and the Individual Retirement Account, which offers two options, the traditional IRA and the Roth IRA. The 401K offers the convenience of a set it and forget it type of setup, while the IRA has the superior tax advantages. Let's take a closer look at each. Be advised that there are other retirement options available, like the 403b and the Roth 401K, but for the sake of this topic we're going to limit our discussion to speaking about the two most common vehicles.

The **401K** is a company sponsored retirement plan that typically comes with a company match of 50-100% on the first 3-5% of employee contributions. That match is free money, never say "no" to free money. The advantage of a 401K is that contributions are tax deferred, meaning that the money that you contribute is not taxed until you withdraw it in retirement. This has the immediate effect of lowering your taxable income and postponing those taxes until retirement, when you will in all probability be in a lower tax bracket. 401K plans are also a convenient and low maintenance way to save for retirement. Once you open the account, you simply select your contribution amount and holding(s) and let it grow. The disadvantages to the plan are that contributions and gains are both taxed at withdrawal and the plans come with administrative fees that can slowly eat away at your gains. Plan options usually come with a selection of 15-25 different funds. The other pitfall of 401K plans is that mutual funds have a reputation for underperforming the market, and as many as 80% of all mutual funds do indeed underperform. On top of that, they come with management fees that can range anywhere from 4% to as high as 10% or more for certain international funds. Sic Figs recommends considering a simple S&P 500 Index fund for your 401K instead.

The management fee on an Index fund will be a fraction of 1% and will return the market average, whatever it happens to be for that particular year. Historically, the S&P 500 returns an average of 8-10% per year. There is no need to hold more than one fund in your 401K. Both mutual funds and index funds are already diversified investments and adding multiple holdings just increases the amount of fees that you pay. In 2024, the contribution limit for employees was $23,000 or $30,500 if you are over 50. Ideally you should contribute a minimum of 12%, if you can afford to do so, but 15% of income should be your target.

The **traditional IRA** is a retirement plan that is independent of your employer, it is one that you set up for yourself. Like the 401K, it has the advantage of using pre-tax dollars to lower your current taxable income. Taxes come out upon withdrawal in retirement, when you should be in a lower tax bracket. The advantage of the IRA over the 401K is that you can invest the money in individual stocks, and not just the 15-25 funds that the typical 401K plan offers. This gives you many more options, but at the same time, that can be overwhelming for someone who knows little or nothing about the stock market. You also need to manage the account yourself, whereas the 401K is more like set it up and let it do its thing. You will need to choose your investments like you would in a normal stock portfolio, accounting for both risk and diversification, and then you will need to account for making the contributions yourself. The maximum annual contribution is also much lower than a 401K, $7,000 in 2024 or $8,000 if you're over 50.

The **Roth IRA** may be the single best retirement account option available to investors. This is because the account is funded with after-tax dollars and because of this, withdrawals taken from a Roth IRA are tax-free, including the gains, as long as it has been at least five years since you made the first contribution to the account. The downside is that the maximum contribution is low, $7,000 or $8,000 over 50. This means that even if you have a Roth IRA or a traditional one for that matter, you will still need another retirement vehicle. The optimal solution is to pair a Roth IRA with your company's 401K plan. You will have to calculate the percentages that work for your particular situation, but make certain that you at least meet the requirements in your 401K contributions to receive the company match. Pairing a Roth IRA and a 401K will also diversify the tax status of your distributions in retirement, as some will be tax deferred and some will be tax free.

CHAPTER 13: CSAS

You cannot underestimate the value of education in building wealth. While there are certainly exceptions to every rule, it is a statistical fact that the more education an individual has, the higher their lifetime earnings potential is going to be. According to data provided by the Motley Fool, high school dropouts earned less than $29,800/year. High school graduates made a shade under $42,590. Associate degrees brought in $55,870 according to the Bureau of Labor Statistics, Bachelor's $80,132, Master's $102,054, Doctoral $141,097 and Professional degrees (medical doctors, lawyers, pharmacists) top it all off at $163,770. Projected over the course of a career, a person with a bachelor's degree will earn about $900,000 more than someone with a high school diploma only. Those with a graduate degree will earn $1.5 million more than those with just a high school diploma.

How about the trades? Plumbers made an average salary of $63,215/year according to the Bureau of Labor Statistics. Electricians $61,391. Hair dresser? The average was $48,422, with the top 10% of earners averaging $61,000. The lowest percentile averaged just $34,000. Truckers averaged $59,925 for company drivers, but the range runs from $47,740-$103,853, depending upon numerous factors. Owner/operators earned as much as $323,899. Carpenters had a mean salary of $63,946. But that is just salary only. Compensation consists of both salary and benefits. A good benefits package can increase one's compensation by more than 20%. The benefits available to an employee are likely to be more attractive as your skill level becomes harder to find and/or replace, meaning that the higher your level of education is, the more specialized your talent becomes, and the more likely you are to be valued and rewarded accordingly. Benefits packages have a value and include essentials such as health insurance, dental insurance, life insurance, paid time off, retirement and pension plans, and other ancillary considerations. When comparing the salaries of trades vs college degrees, it's important to note that many trades people operate as independent contractors, receiving little if anything in the way of benefits. For example, the carpenter making $63,000 a year and receiving no benefits is bringing in $63,000 per year in compensation. But the person with a bachelor's degree earning $80,000 a year and pairing that with an attractive benefits package is actually bringing home upwards of $100,000 per year in total compensation. This demonstrates the lifetime advantage of having a higher level of education for the average person and shows that a side by side comparison of salaries is misleading. Again, these are the averages. There are always exceptions and outliers to every set of statistics. All of this is not to say that everyone has to go to college, but this is a book about wealth building and getting rich. It's no coincidence that the wealthier segment of society also happens to be the most educated. I like to use an example from my own personal life experience. My mom had four children, two have college degrees and two do not. One of those four is a one percenter, another is a two percenter, and the other two are not even sniffing the top 50% in terms of wealth. Which ones do you think have more money? Yeah, it's the college educated ones. Success, and I mean *real* success, sits at the confluence of all of the smart decisions that you make for yourself. You need to put yourself in a position to be successful, and that means work ethic, investing, debt management, living to be successful and education. It doesn't just happen. Having said that, the key is to start early, and that means opening a **College Savings Account** for your child. This will allow you to set them up for a greater level of success later on.

CSAs come in two options. The 529 account and the Coverdell education savings account. CSAs work much the same way that the retirement accounts that we've already discussed work, with the 529 being similar in form and function to the 401K and the Coverdell operating like an IRA. I'm just going to come out and say it. Don't bother with the Coverdell. Your best bet for saving money towards your child's future education is the 529 plan. Coverdell CSAs cap at $2,000 in contributions per year. You have to account for and remember to fund the account every year. And just like the IRA, you can invest in whatever individual company stock that suits your fancy. Sounds good, but unless you are a stock picking guru, you are better off sticking with the "managed for you" 529. The distributions in the Coverdell are tax free as long as they do not exceed the beneficiary's qualified educational expense. A 529 plan runs much the same way that a 401K does. Each state offers their own plan, but they can also be set up through a broker or financial institution like Vanguard or Fidelity Investments. With a 529 plan, you can arrange for contributions to be taken directly from your paycheck each pay period, although there is no employer match here, like with the 401K. Plans tend to have 15-25 funds to choose from and the savings grow tax deferred. Withdrawals are tax free as long as they are used for qualified educational expenses. Contribution limits run around $18,000 per year, making it a better option for covering college expenses than the $2,000 per year Coverdell. The main disadvantage to a 529 plan is that it can affect how much financial aid that your student qualifies for. Also, the funds come with management fees, unlike the Coverdell, where you hold individual stocks. When setting up a 529 plan, stick to the index funds for their lower fee structures.

CHAPTER 14:
PARTING SHOTS

Everything in this book so far has been a series of suggestions that you can use in consideration when putting together and managing your own portfolio and wealth building strategy, but there is one last thing that I want to talk about to all of the future 1 and 2 percenters out there, and it's something that I tell my daughter constantly. **Don't talk about your money and never tell anyone how much you're worth.** Why not? Because it's just not a good idea on so many levels. First of all, it's nobody's business and it should never be a part of any conversation that you have. You will simply set yourself up to be judged based upon a whole preconceived set of notions and expectations. And it could be dangerous.

For starters, you will never know who is being open, honest and genuine with you, and who simply wants to get their hands on your cash. Put simply, you may never be able to figure out who your real friends are. Success breeds jealousy. Some people may want to "borrow" money from you or ask you to co-sign a loan for them. You may get asked to invest in some fly-by-night opportunity that someone is involved in, like a start-up business or invention. I've personally been asked to pay for schooling. None of these things are good ideas by the way, and they may hold it against you when you say no. You might also find that you are the "go to" whenever somebody needs money, or be expected to pay for things, like when you go out for dinner with friends and family. Expectations may be set unreasonably high for

Christmas and Birthday presents, leading to disappointment and resentment. Look, it's okay to be generous. I'm not saying that it isn't. But do you really want the expectation to be set for you, without your consent or input? Or do you want to be the one who decides what is appropriate to the given situation?

On the darker side of things, letting people know your net worth can set you up to be targeted by criminals, either in cyberspace, by home intrusion or physical assault, like a mugging or robbery. This does not mean and is not intended to suggest that you can't enjoy the benefits of the wealth that you have built for yourself. By all means, take advantage. Just be cognizant of the potential ramifications of announcing it to the world at large. I personally like the freedom of enjoying the things that make me happy in private. I buy new cars, I wear luxury watches when I go out, I like to eat at fancy restaurants and stay in expensive hotels. But I don't talk about it or post it all over social media. No one needs to know but me and those that operate in my inner circle. Having said that, it's your money. Do what feels right to you. If you're rich, you've got options. And having options is the whole point of this book.

CHAPTER 15: PRACTICAL APPLICATIONS

Now it's your turn to try your hand at identifying the entry and exit points of the given stock charts. Find support and resistance for the examples given and then compare your answers to the given data.

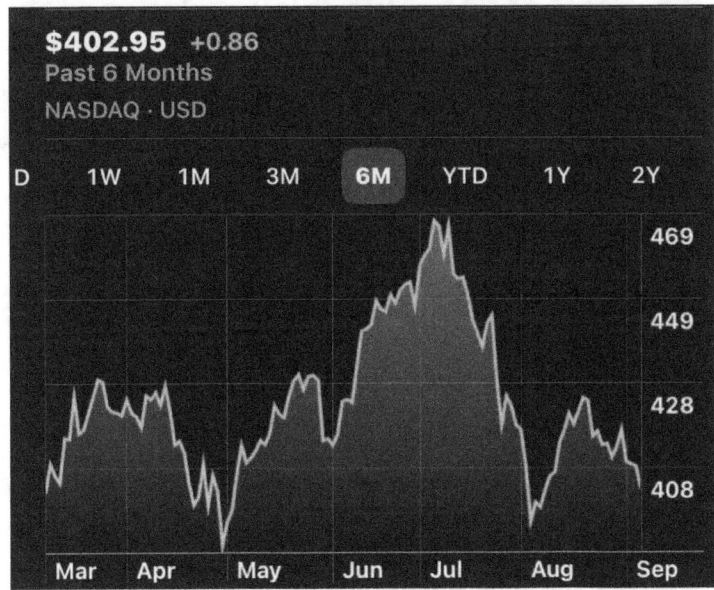

Your answer:

Support:_____**Resistance:**_____

Sic Figs answer taken from pinpoint data provided by Yahoo

Finance pegs support at $396.55 and resistance at $500.00.

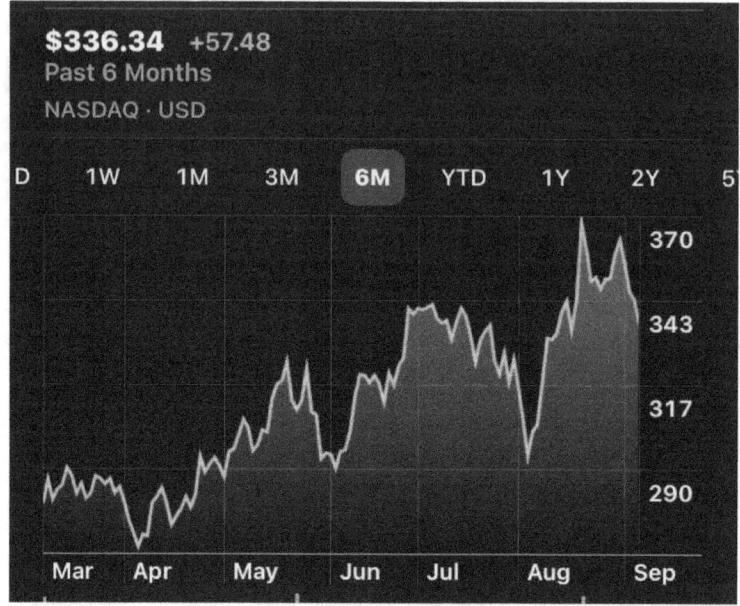

Your answer:

Support:_____**Resistance:**_____

Sic Figs answer taken from pinpoint data provided by Yahoo Finance has support at $296.83 and resistance at $377.00.

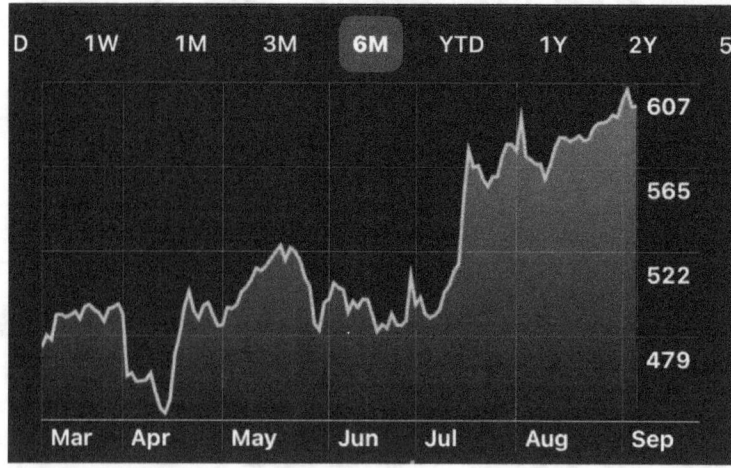

Your answer:

Support:_____**Resistance:**_____

Sic Figs answer taken from pinpoint data provided by Yahoo Finance has support at $488.27 and resistance at $600.00

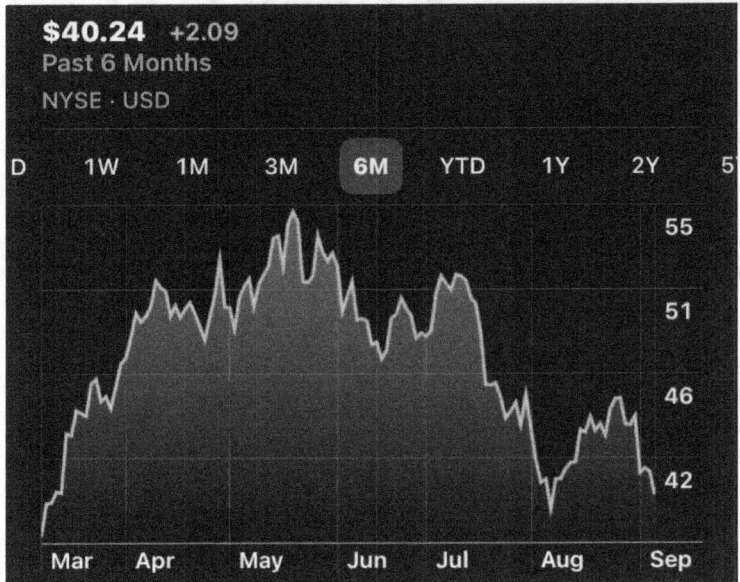

Your answer:

Support:_____**Resistance:**_____

Sic Figs answer based on pinpoint data provided by Yahoo Finance has support at $39.94 and resistance at $52.77.

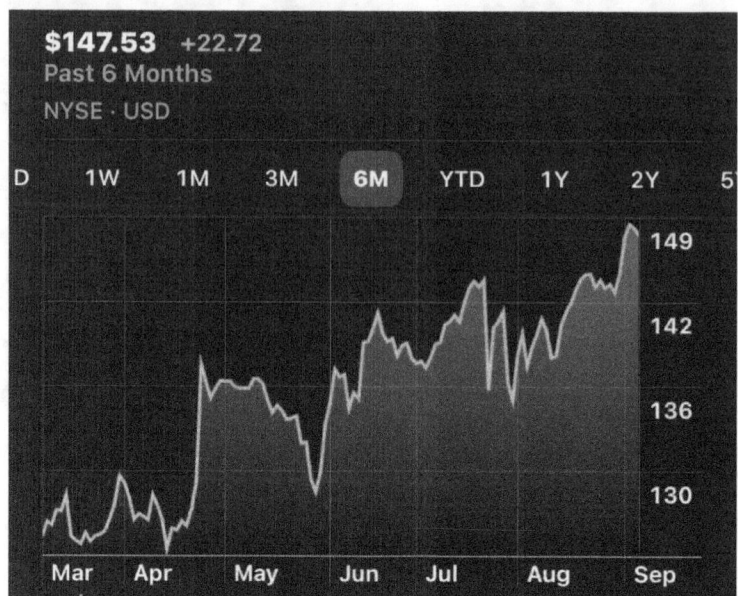

Your answer:

Support:_____**Resistance:**_____

Sic Figs answer based on pinpoint data provided by Yahoo Finance has support at $138.71 and resistance at $147.60.

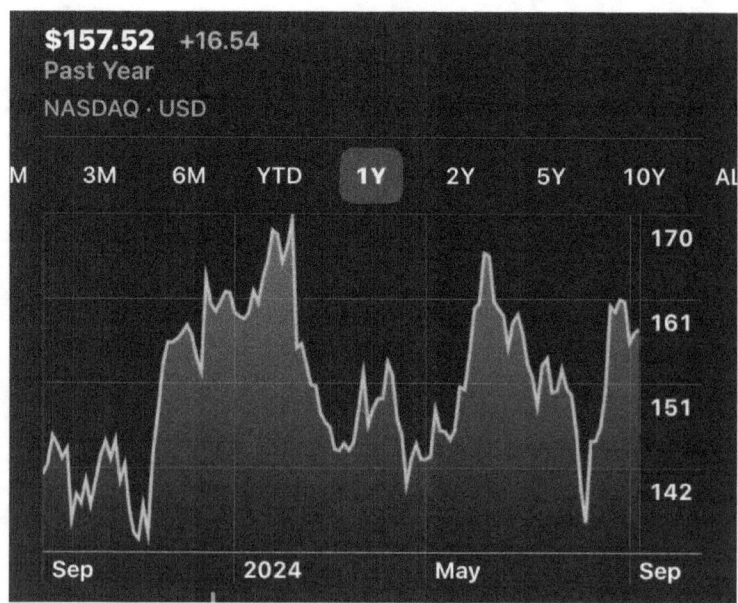

Your answer:

Support:_____**Resistance:**_____

Sic Figs answer based on pinpoint data provided by Yahoo Finance has support at $135.29 and resistance at $161.91.

Buy, Sell or Hold

Review the stock charts below and determine if each is a buy, a sell, or a hold.

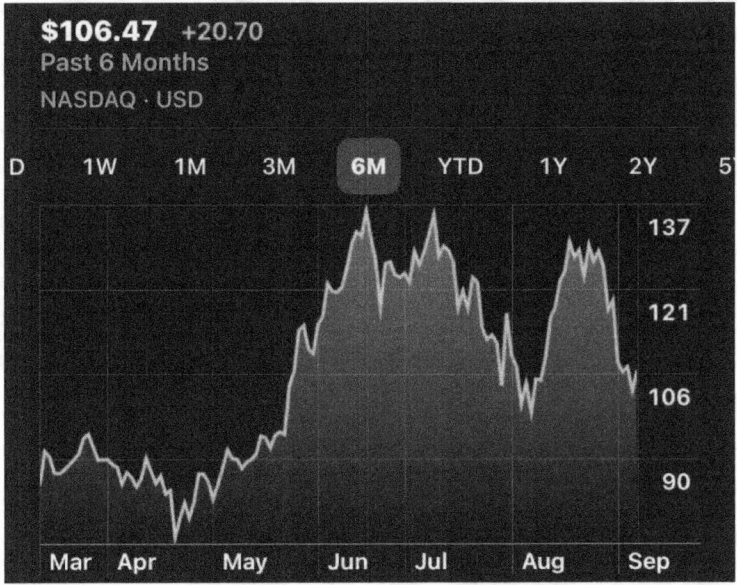

Your call:

Buy. Since dipping in April, this stock has established a support line at $106 and has held it three times. It did begin to form an inflection point starting in June with a series of lower and lower highs, but the dip has been realized and support held. Sic Figs would rate this stock as a buy.

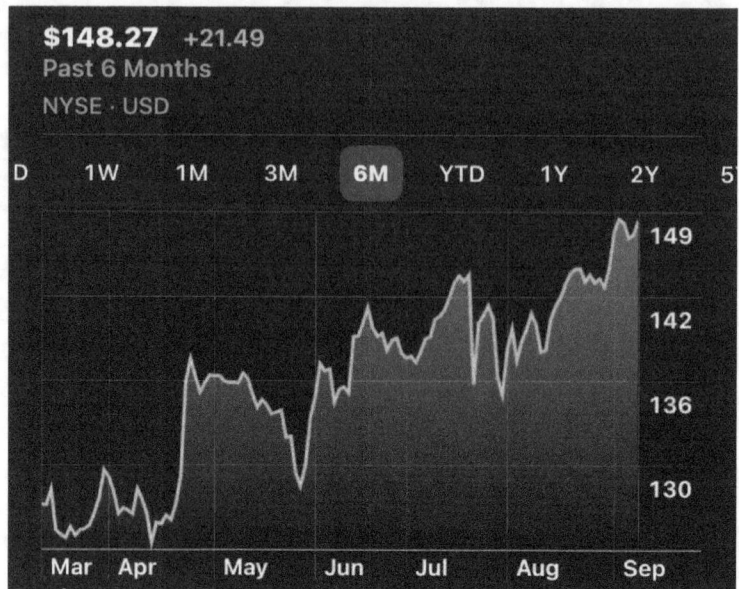

Your call:

Buy. This stock is showing the classic bull pattern of higher highs and higher lows. Sic Figs would rate this stock as a buy, but note that it is significantly off support. A better entry point, closer to $140 would be optimal.

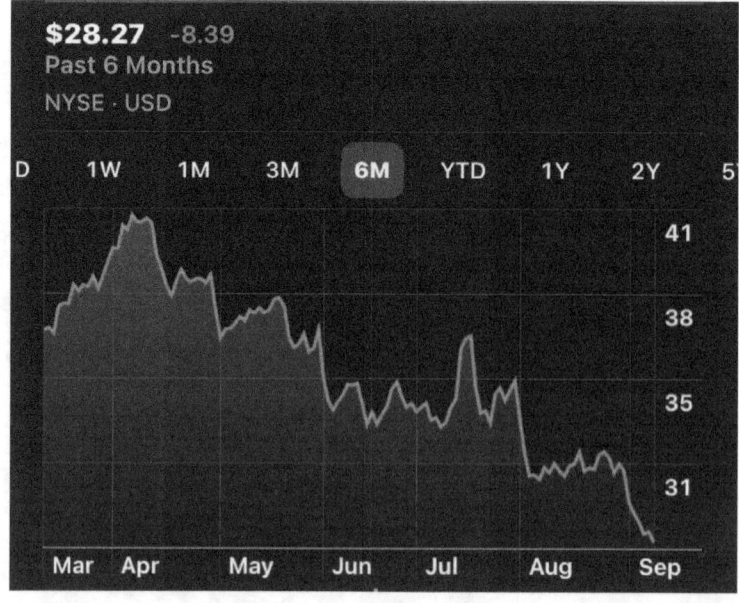

Your call:

Sell. This is just as obvious as the example in the above chart, this is a screaming sell, as indicated by its continuous pattern of lower highs and lower lows. It has failed to hold multiple levels of support.

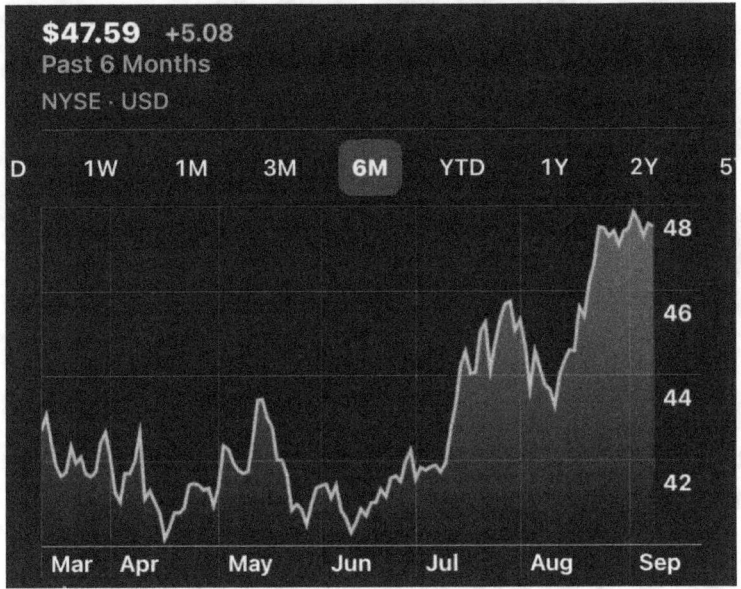

Your call:

Sell. Strictly speaking, this stock is bullish. But it has also broken through resistance . You would do well to wait for a pullback before adding it to your portfolio.

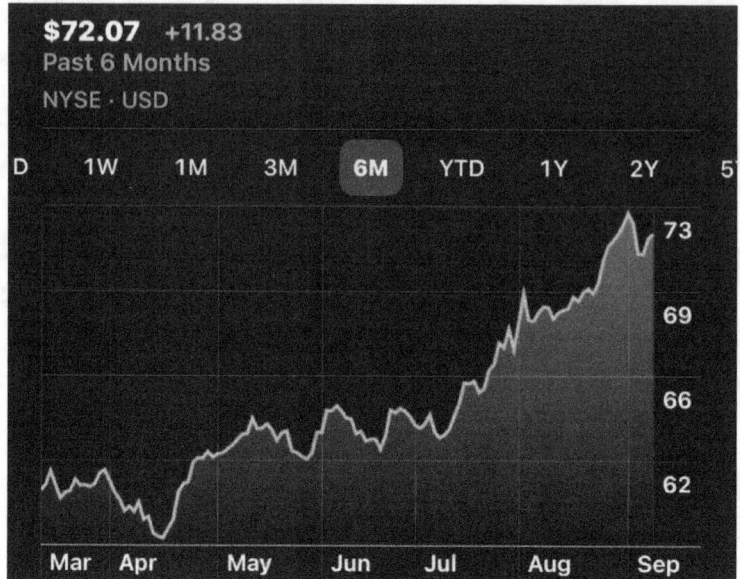

Your call:

Sell. Again, this is a bullish stock. But it has broken through resistance not once, but twice! Stocks like these will eventually return to their mean. This is also a defensive stock. During a rotation to growth, this stock will sell off hard. Just like with violations of support, where it becomes the new resistance, once a stock breaks resistance, that line becomes the new support. In this example, the new line of support rests at $66.75.

Your call:

Buy. You could argue that this stock is trending towards an inflection point, with a trend towards lower highs forming over a two-month interval, but it has also withstood four tests on support.

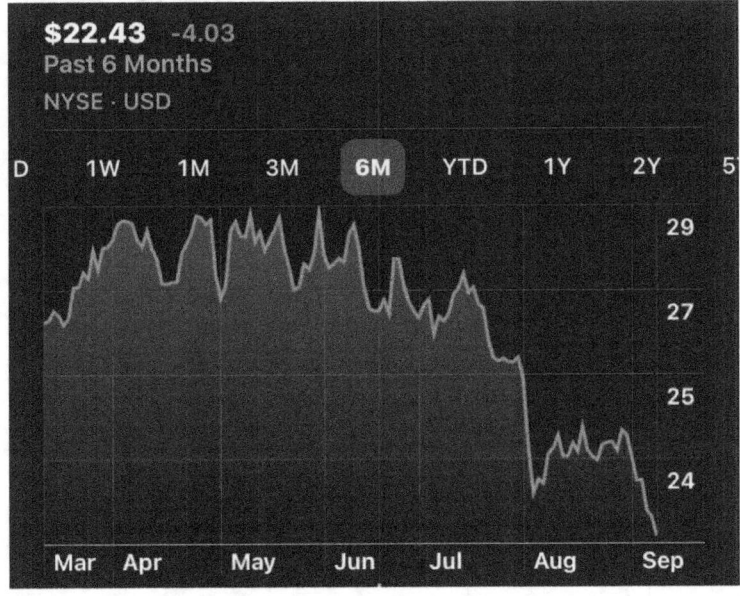

Your call:

Sell. Lower lows, lower highs. Multiple violations of support. There is no redeeming factor to this chart.

Your Call:

Buy. Despite the early August dip, which was a strong broad-market sell-off, this stock has reliably held support on eight different occasions.

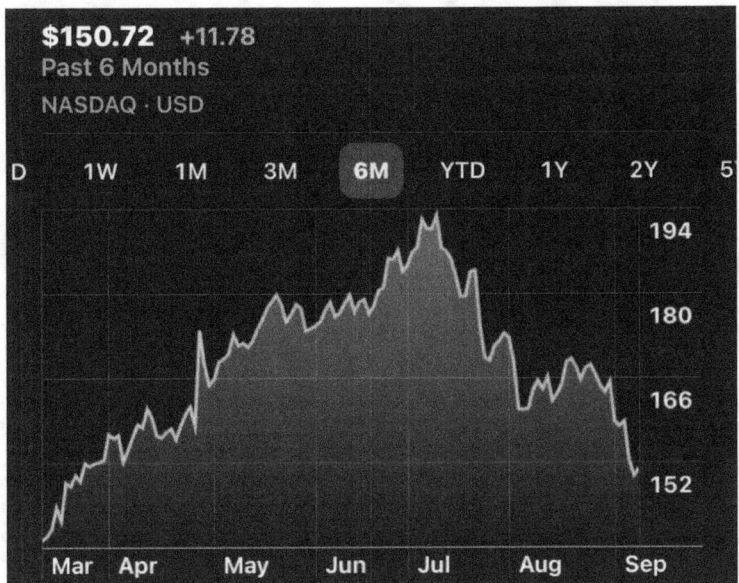

Your call:

Sell. This stock has broken through support after bouncing from it four different times. However, this is a high quality company, so if you were looking for an opportunity to initiate a position you could refer to the 12-month chart, where it has held support (seen below).

As shown, it is an opportunity at this level if your investing time frame is longer.

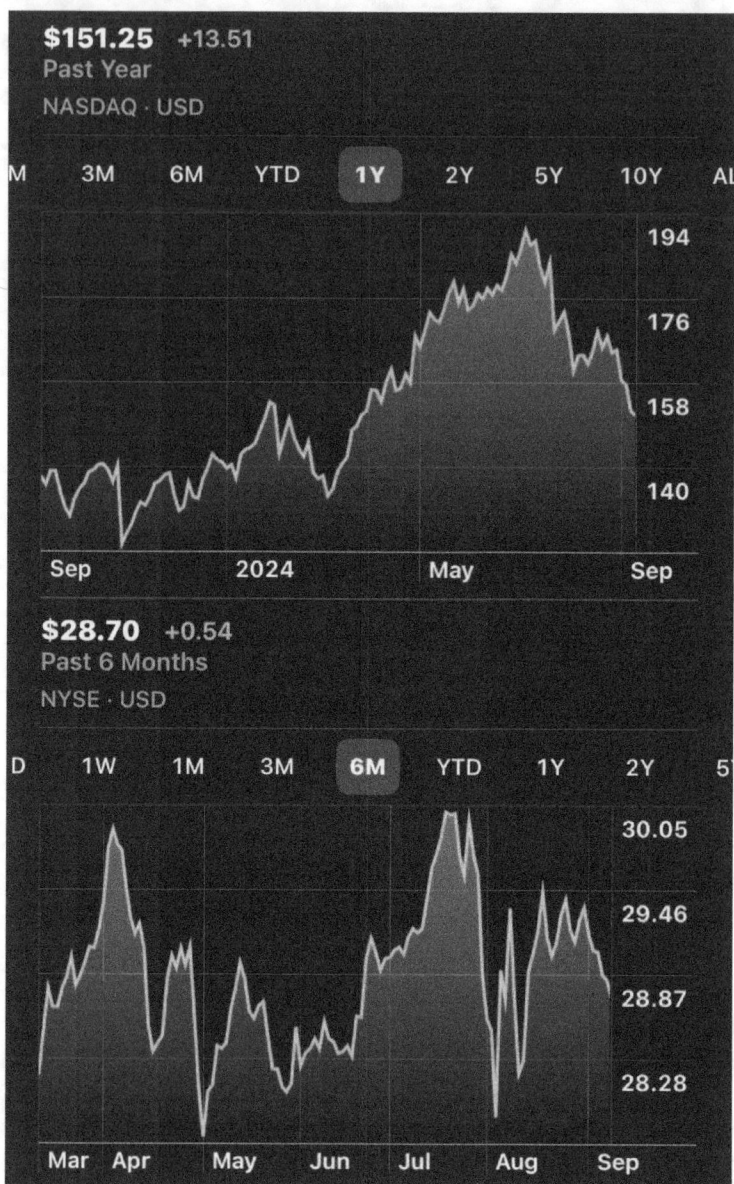

$151.25 +13.51
Past Year
NASDAQ · USD

$28.70 +0.54
Past 6 Months
NYSE · USD

Your call:

Hold. Overall, this is a bullish stock, with a support line showing a mild upward trajectory. But the price action is given to swinging wildly and the highs have been trending lower. A return to the support line seems inevitable. There are better options for your money.

Visit Sic Figs on Facebook for ideas, inspiration and news affecting the stock market and your portfolio.
https://www.facebook.com/sicfigs

SIC FIGS VS S&P 500

Returns:

2008 42% vs -37%
2009 36% vs 26.5%
2010 37% vs 12.8%
2011 -12% vs flat
2012   4% vs 13.4%
2013 -22% vs 29.6%
2014 18% vs 11.4%
2015 35% vs -.073%
2016 19% vs 9.54%
2017 25% vs 19.4%
2018 -3% vs -6.24%
2019 2.4% vs 28.9%
2020 19% vs 16.3%
2021 11% vs 26.9%
2022 -26% vs -19.4%
2023 22% vs 24.2%

ABOUT THE AUTHOR

Donald Smyth

Donald Smyth is the admin and primary contributor to the Sic Figs investment ideas social media platform found on Facebook and TikTok. He has been an avid investor in stocks for nearly twenty years and is the author of the wilderness suspense thriller The Alpha of Purgatory, the young adult murder mystery A Night in the Mangroves and the sci-fi dystopian novel Sixth of Ten.

BOOKS BY THIS AUTHOR

The Alpha Of Purgatory

When a man living off the grid in the remote Purgatory Valley with a pack of orphaned wolves reluctantly teams up with the head of a conservation effort aimed at restoring the gray wolf population of Yellowstone National Park, they unwittingly become entangled in a violent conspiracy determined to derail the reintroduction plan by murdering the plan's administrator.

A Night In The Mangroves

Three young teenage friends go camping on a deserted island sitting off the coast of the Florida Keys, only to find themselves being tormented by an unseen threat as nightfall drops a curtain of darkness over the isolated landscape. Who's stalking the boys and what do they want? That will be the mystery that two detectives will try to unravel forty years later when they are called upon to investigate the discovery of two skeletons found hidden beneath a small, overturned boat in the densely overgrown interior of the private island known as Shands Key.

Sixth Of Ten

He's just won the lottery! But she's just been assigned to kill him. When a narcoleptic and disfigured teenager wins the annual State-sponsored death lottery he makes a run for the border of the nearest country that offers asylum to lottery winners, traveling along a modern-day underground railroad and pursued by his

State assigned assasin, who will stop at nothing to make sure that he fulfills his onerous and deadly obligation.

YOU VS THE S&P 500

AFTERWORD

Having wealth was perhaps best summed up by the Roman Emperor Nero after he built his golden palace on top of the ruins that followed in the wake of the great fire of Rome in 64 A.D. "I can finally start living like a human being," he said. It is interesting in that in the times that we now find ourselves, it is getting harder and harder to "live like a human being," especially when you consider inflation and what it has done to the cost of every day essentials such as food, housing, energy and just about anything really that makes your life more pleasant and enjoyable. Never let anyone tell you that you're rich enough. Because the rest of the world is coming for you.

Donald Smyth- October 29, 2023

ACKNOWLEDGEMENT

First of all, I want to offer a great big Thank You to everyone who purchased, downloaded or otherwise supported the release of my debut novel, The Alpha of Purgatory. I owe you both a great debt of gratitude...Yes, I'm joking.

I especially want to thank everyone who took the time to leave a review of one of my books on Amazon and Goodreads. Reviews are the lifeblood of the undiscovered author, helping to generate a little chatter and momentum for works that no one is specifically looking for, or even aware of until they stumble upon your generous words. Reviews also influence the algorithms that determine where a book lands in a product search, so they are more important than you may even know.

Special thanks to Samantha Smyth for executing her editing prowess on my behalf on this and all of the books that I write. These books wouldn't be nearly as good without her assistance. Follow me at:

https://www.facebook.com/TheAlphaofPurgatory
https://www.amazon.com/author/donald.ballou.smyth

www.ingramcontent.com/pod-product-compliance
Lightning Source LLC
Chambersburg PA
CBHW062358290526
45794CB00010B/690